Quotable Pop

Five Decades of Blah Blah Blah

by
Phil Dellio & Scott Woods

Caricatures by
Mike Rooth

Quotable Books

Table of Contents

Also by Phil Dellio & Scott Woods

I Wanna Be Sedated:
Pop Music in the Seventies
Caricatures by Dave Prothero
isbn 0-920151-16-7

This Is How We Do It

Every kid hears it growing up. It's the all-purpose escape hatch for parents who fall short of their own prescribed rules: "Do as I say, not as I do." For most parents, it works pretty well. But if the speaker were David Lee Roth or Courtney Love or Jerry Lee Lewis, where the saying is sometimes even more morally dubious than the doing, some poor kid might get the wrong idea. If you were David Lee Roth's son, you'd do well to be wary of all fatherly advice not accompanied by an outright disclaimer: "Don't do as I do, and definitely don't do as I say—in fact, don't pay any attention to me at all."

But pop stars do say a lot of funny things, and we believe you're holding one of the funniest books about pop music ever published (which modesty allows us to say, because we didn't actually write it). Sometimes they mean to be funny, sometimes they're funny accidentally. You'll find a mix of both herein, and we'll leave it to you to sort out which is which. With Neil Young, Stevie Wonder, Bruce Springsteen, and lots of other important people who are either underrepresented or not represented at all in what follows, it's because they usually fell somewhere in between in whatever interviews we came across: too thoughtful, or too guarded, or just not amusing enough for our purposes. There are interview and quote books other than ours that do a much better job at compiling thoughtful introspection. But when it comes to the heroes of this book (and we'll tip our hand a little bit here)—Bob Dylan, Snoop Doggy Dogg, the Pet Shop Boys, Madonna, Homer Simpson, and the four very quick-witted lads fielding questions at a typical Beatles press conference circa 1964—their words translate as great pop music, sometimes as sublime as the real thing.

We tried to provide a date for as many of the quotes we've collected as possible, and by our estimate we got about 95% of them. They're culled from numerous sources, a complete list of which can be found at the back of the book. Especially helpful were *Jabberrock, Off the Record, Rolling Stone Raves, The Lost Beatles Interviews,* and *The Superstars in Their Own Words* in the book department; and *Creem, Spin, Playboy, Select, Q, Graffiti,* and *Nerve!* among periodicals. For the sake of readability, we favoured quotes that could stand alone without any accompanying or parenthetical explanation. To facilitate this, we occasionally substitute a name, song title, or album title for an unidentified pronoun—e.g., "Right Said Fred changed the course of history" instead of "They changed the course of history," followed by a note explaining who "they" are—taking great care not to alter the speaker's intent in any way.

A word of warning, especially if you've lost touch with the popular music press over the past decade: in the course of saying funny things, musicians occasionally use language and broach subjects that you don't want either your kids or your grandmother to read. Most of these quotes are found in two sections in particular— one's about sex, and it's very sexual; the other's about penises, and it contains quotes about penises—but there are others scattered about. We tried not to go beyond the pale; when necessary, we stepped in and protected some of these people from themselves.

Open up and dive in anywhere. Being very alphabet-conscious, we start with ABBA.

* * *

A few acknowledgements:

Phil Dellio — Just for sort of being around, thanks to Edith Bartlett, Chris Buck, Chris Cook, Renée Crist, Peter and Patricia Dellio, Chuck Eddy, staff and students at Huttonville P.S., Norm Ibuki, Steve Keslick, Dave MacIntosh, Dianne Mann, Pam Martin, Sandra Novak, Jeff Pike, Dave and Julie Porter, Tim Powis, Richard Riegel, Mike Saunders, Brent Sclisizzi, Rob Sheffield, Peter Stephens, Alastair Sutherland, Cam Victor, Justin Zachariah, and Alan Zweig. And, of course, Scott Woods.

Scott Woods — A whole bunch of people to thank: Tom Sawyer and Paul Woods for letting me raid their bookshelves, and the rest of my family for offering steady encouragement along the way (sorry about the language, mom); Dave Bookman, Chris Buck, Bryce Johnson, Frank Kogan, Lucas Mulder, Dave Newfeld, and Steven Ward for putting up with me all these years; Stuart Berman, Chuck Eddy, and Brian O'Connor for publishing (and paying) me on more than one occasion; folks too numerous to mention at the HMV Superstore in Toronto, the best place in the world to talk shop; Phil Dellio for five months of blah blah blah (and then some); Jacqueline Baines for changing my life, something pop music almost never does anymore.

Both of us would like to thank Geoff Savage at Sound And Vision for initiating this project and carrying it through with enthusiasm and dedication; David Barber, Mike Walsh, and Jonathan Savage for helpful input along the way; Mike Rooth for all the great illustrations; and all the unnamed critics, authors, and reporters whose questions set most of what you're about to read in motion.

Phil Dellio & Scott Woods

WE'LL TAKE SWEDEN
(ABBA)

"I wanted a name that would put us first in the phone directory, or second if you count ABBA."

—Martin Fry, ABC

"I remember hearing 'SOS' on the radio in the States and realizing that it was ABBA. But it was too late, because I was already transported by it."
—Pete Townshend, 1982

"ABBA hardly ever lay a turkey on you. They've kind of hit a rut these days, but they were in there just blammin' 'em onto the charts for ages, which is admirable. Also, the girls are nice looking!"

—Joe Strummer, the Clash, 1981

"ABBA sound meaner to me than any of those idiot punk groups."

—Nick Lowe, 1982

"Thanks, everybody! It's really a great pleasure to play here. One of my favorite groups of all time is ABBA. ABBA!!"

—Bob Dylan, 1991

YOU ARE A WALKING ANTIQUE
(AGE)

"Um, 28. No, I'm 27...I'll be 28 next year. Want a clam?"

—Kenny MacLean, Platinum Blonde, 1986

"Nobody's too old to rock 'n' roll, but there is a difference between being 40 and being 30."

—Ian Anderson, Jethro Tull, 1978

"I think I'm going to die when I'm 30. I don't know why, I've just got this feeling about it. That's why I try to live each day as fully as I can."

—Robbie Williams, 1997

"I used to be afraid of being in my 40s. Now I find out my 40s are pretty good. Of course, I'm rich and I'm married to Christie Brinkley. And that will tend to skew one's view of things."

—Billy Joel, 1993

"I'll grow old physically, but I won't grow old musically."

—Cliff Richard, 1980

"I don't want to be one of these middle-aged guys who turns up with the baseball hat on the wrong way around."

—Elvis Costello, 1994

"With a lot of the things I did on *Doggystyle*, I was just being a youngster growing up, and now I'm more of the father-type figure."

—Snoop Doggy Dogg, 1996

"I got to thinking, what more can music do for me? I had a number one hit for myself so what would I get out of it? Another number one hit? A bigger ranch? So what. I play 'Old Macdonald' on my guitar for my daughter, but that's about it."

—Terry Jacks, 1989

"Elvis Presley said, 'You're not going to marry this little girl, are you? This is a joke, isn't it?' I said, 'No, I'm going to marry her.' And he said, 'Well, God bless you, Jerry Lee. You just saved my career.'"

—Jerry Lee Lewis, 1988

"It would be great if we could get rid of the Rock and Roll Hall of Fame and actually have some quality-control guys going around saying, 'O.K., you've got one more record: Mean it or go!'"

—Robert Plant, 1993

"I don't see any reason why there has to be an age limit to performing rap; there's no age limit in rock. For fuck's sake, look at Kiss!"

—Ice-T, 1995

"Colleges are like old-age homes; except for the fact that more people die in colleges than in old-age homes, there's really no difference."

—Bob Dylan, 1966

COULD'VE BEEN THE WHISKEY, MIGHT'VE BEEN THE GIN
(ALCOHOL)

"I stopped drinking in June. It's been reported that I gave up drinking over the previous Christmas, but that's not the case. I'm not stupid enough to try and stop drinking over Christmas."

—Graham Coxon, Blur, 1997

"I got highly drunk on Monday night and did the usual things—said things I didn't mean, made friends I don't want, made enemies I don't need."

—Martin Carr, Boo Radleys, 1996

"I'm a total beer slob."

—Sheryl Crow, 1998

"I used to put orange juice in vodka. That's what I had for breakfast during my last two years of high school. Just to get through the first and second period."

—Steven Tyler, Aerosmith, 1975

"A hangover is a cure, not an illness. They're good. If you're having less than four or five a week, you should increase your alcohol intake drastically."

—Clive Jackson, Doctor and the Medics, 1988

"We used to drink more whisky, but for drinking in quantity we found it's a lot less damaging to drink wine. Would you like to come out one Friday night and get drunk with us?"

—Roger Earl, Foghat, 1978

"I like me voice at the moment. It's rockin'! Just go to bed at night, that's all. If you don't go to bed at night you'll get a sore throat. I don't take throat lozenges or drink honey and goat's fuckin' essence or any of that shit. I just smoke cigarettes, drink Jack Daniel's a lot, and feel fuckin' great!"

—Liam Gallagher, Oasis, 1997

"Hearing a record of mine on the air for the first time was the closest I ever came to being drunk."

—Pat Boone, 1988

"I never get drunk. Two drinks and I get a headache and fall asleep."

—Lou Reed, 1975

ZOOROPA
(ANIMALS)

"I can't believe these journalists, asking you about your dogs and shit. 'Is it true you get into bed with your dogs naked?' Catch this: dogs are *always* naked."

—Snoop Doggy Dogg, 1996

"You have to be careful about control. It's like when you take a bunch of chickens to the park and you try to keep them all together and you're yelling, 'Hey! Chicken! Come back here!' so that when you finally get the chickens corralled, they all die of heat exhaustion."

—Tom Waits, 1994

"I mainly like 'Ben' as a record. I love rats. And I like it as a friend, too, as if I'm talking to a guy that's a friend of mine—but none other than just a friend! Some people see it the rat way. Some people see it the friend way. It works both ways."

—Michael Jackson, 1977

4

"I know how people work. And they're a lot more bizarre than shrimps."

—Robyn Hitchcock, 1988

"I was really into Sparks for two years until the singer said there were two things in the world that he didn't like, animals and children, and that really hurt me."

—Björk, 1994

NEVER MIND THE POLLOCKS
(ART)

"It's not art in the same way as painting a picture."

—Keith Emerson, ELP, 1974

"I love photography. I photographed children for a long time. And buildings...I'm beginning to sound like David Byrne."

—Michael Stipe, R.E.M., 1992

"David Byrne would qualify as an artist. I mean, by appearance's sake. He looks like he's dying."

—David Lee Roth, 1981

"We don't think in terms of history or art. Art is in the eyes of the beholder. Is it art if people get off on your music? It doesn't really matter, does it?"

—John Hannah, Streetheart, 1979

"The arguments of kids with older people? Hell, that's nothing new. We didn't invent it. I was thinking, you know, that it's possible that Michelangelo's folks said to him, 'Look, we don't want you to be an artist, so shape up, kid, and get a haircut!' No, really, seriously, it's possible."

—Brian Cole, the Association, 1968

"I didn't understand one thing Salvador Dali said. He speaks three languages that I don't speak. All we understood is that we didn't understand each other. He likes that. He's into total confusion. He says I'm his favorite example of total confusion."

—Alice Cooper, 1973

"I had a very excellent art teacher, Peter Frampton's father, who was an inspiration to all who were involved with him."

—David Bowie, 1988

"I'm just soooo abstract! I'm so Jackson Pollock. Talking a load of old Pollocks! It's All! A Load! Of Pollocks!"

—Beth Orton, 1999

"They always say that Jane's Addiction is some sort of art students' band. When I first heard that, I got mad. Like, I went, 'Hey, we're no art school band, we never went to art school.' And I thought about that and fuck, I would love to be in art school right now, at this present time. Talking about the parties on the weekend, going to clay class, sitting down behind the wheel, it's time to go to the next class, listening to Hendrix records, discussing the Sugarcubes. 'Who's better, the Sugarcubes or the Pixies?' 'No, no, no. It's Guns N' Roses.' 'Oh, have you heard Jane's Addiction?' That's a tough life."

—Perry Farrell, Jane's Addiction, 1988

MORE QUOTES ABOUT BUILDINGS AND FOOD
(AVANT-GARDE)

"The Ramones and Talking Heads toured England together in a cold bus in '76, sulking the whole way. The intellectual Heads wanted to visit Stonehenge and museums, which appalled the unhappy Ramones, who just wanted to find hamburgers. When the Heads started speaking French, the Ramones plunged to the depths of misery and horror."

—Tom Verlaine, Television, 1995

"I remember sitting at the same table with Iggy Pop and Lou Reed, listening to them not talk to each other."

—David Byrne, Talking Heads, 1995

"To me, 'The Brady Bunch' is completely avant-garde. It's out there!"

—Vernon Reid, Living Colour, 1988

"In retrospect it is hard to take stock of it. I mean, going down to the Electric Ballroom and hitting empty film cans and scratching a guitar about, playing this jittering, apologetic half-reggae and singing about hegemony while putting in as many discords as you could was probably doomed to failure, I suppose."

—Green Gartside, Scritti Politti, 1985

"I consider myself responsible for a whole new school of pretensions—they know who they are. Don't you, Elton? Just kidding. No, I'm not. See what I mean? That was a thoroughly pretentious statement."

—David Bowie, 1976

WHY DO WORDS SUDDENLY APPEAR?
(BACHARACH & DAVID)

"When you say the name Burt Bacharach, right away it triggers off love melodies, harmonies, beautiful records, incredible songs that he wrote with Hal David. Know what I mean? That's a source of love, right there, Burt Bacharach is. His name is. He might not be in that frame of mind today, but his name is always in that frame of mind. Know what I mean?"

—Brian Wilson, 1988

"At first I thought of doing this tour without makeup. But then I decided it had to be done more gradually. I mean, with dancers whirling around and Vincent Price doing a monologue about spiders on the P.A., I didn't want the kids to get the idea that my first love, Burt Bacharach, was lurking in the wings!"

—Alice Cooper, 1975

"For song styling, I'd say Sinatra. On the female side, Peggy Lee and Aretha. But if you're talking about really heavy people—heavy, heavy, heavy— I'd say Burt Bacharach."

—James Brown, 1991

"The other thing that I really enjoyed were the early compositions of David and Bacharach. I thought that they were so good because prior to that time there had been little of bitonal or polytonal harmonic implication in American pop music, and we are to thank them for providing that through those early Dionne Warwick recordings."

—Frank Zappa, 1987

HANGING ON IN QUIET DESPERATION IS THE ENGLISH WAY
(BRIT-SPEAK)

"Oh, you've arrived at the perfect time. The tea and cakes have just come."

—Steve Strange, Visage, 1981

"I'm mad for Easy Listening. Double mad. Sergio Mendes, all that stuff."

—Bonehead, Oasis, 1995

"You know, the English can say 'marvelous' pretty good. They can't say 'raunchy' so good, though."

—Bob Dylan, 1966

"Sex? I'd rather have a cup of tea."

—Boy George, 1983

REPORTER: What are some of your hip words in England?
JOHN LENNON: They're ever changing, you know, madam. 'Alec Douglas,' that's a big one. 'Wilson,' everybody does it."

—1964

"We've played many palaces, including Frisco's Cow Palace. But never this one before. It's a keen pad and I like the staff. Thought they'd be dukes and things but they were just fellas."

—Paul McCartney on Buckingham Palace, 1965

WE COME FROM THE LAND OF THE ICE AND SNOW
(CANADA)

"It's BTO—they're Canada's answer to ELP. Their big hit was 'TCB.' That's how we talked in the '70s. We didn't have a moment to spare."

—Homer Simpson, 2000

"Canadian content's a drag. It's great for Anne Murray, Gordon Lightfoot, and the Guess Who. They go waltzing along with these Edward Bear things. What has Canadian content done for BTO, Crowbar, April Wine, Mahogany Rush...?"
—Randy Bachman, 1974

"Loverboy? They make me ashamed to be a Canadian, them in their 30's and still crying about some hot chick."
—Ivan Doroschuk, Men Without Hats, 1983

"Bands with images are way up my butt. Skinny Puppy in particular were annoying because they behaved like little children when the gear didn't quite measure up to their standard. Right. I'll bet you guys are so fucking huge up in the Great White that you get exactly what you want, every time."
—Steve Albini, 1985

"You Canadians are so easy to please. You should hear what I say about you in the States."
—Billy Bragg, 1985

"I've always wanted to live in Canada. But hey, keep this under your cap. I'm saving Canada for when we really get in trouble."
—Chuck D, Public Enemy, 1988

"If people want to compare BTO with the Guess Who, I'd like them to do it on a higher level and not in the smut we can say about each other, because I could really lay some neat things on you about them."
—Randy Bachman, 1975

"I'll always remember Toronto, because they've got a radio station called CHUM, and that's what I feed my dog."
—Nick Heyward, 1988

WE'RE ON A MISSION, YOU BETTER JUST LISTEN
(CAUSES)

"We're not up there to, like, save the whales or anything, you know."

—Jay Hanson, 1998

"I believe that rock 'n' roll has saved the world. It's prevented World War Three. Too many people ignore what rock has done for the world. But really, man, rock 'n' roll has saved us all from total destruction."

—Jerry Nolan, New York Dolls, 1973

"I want to wear my beliefs. I want to get ANIMAL RIGHTS tattooed on the back of my neck. One time I really wanted to get REJECT tattooed across my forehead. Now I want to write LOVE on my hand, just to remind me that that's a good thing to do."

—Moby, 1995

NEIL TENNANT: What I don't like is when pop stars behave like, "Hey! Listen kids! We know something you don't know! The ozone layer's really screwed up! It's, like, terrible! You shouldn't use aerosol deodorants!" EVERYONE IN THE WORLD knows that. It's like when pop stars are against war: "Listen! We're all against war! It's a really bad thing!" As if people think, "Oh, we think war's fantastic, actually, but I've now changed my mind because John Lennon's told me peace is a good thing."
CHRIS LOWE: He's enough to make you want to go to war, John Lennon...

—Pet Shop Boys, 1989

"I'm for nuclear power, but I haven't told anyone because I am still hoping to fuck Jane Fonda like everybody dreams of doing who's involved in the No Nuke Movement."

—Pete Townshend, 1980

"How can anyone in the world shoot a rhino when there's only a thousand left?"

—Mike Tramp, White Lion, 1989

"If there is any politics in the Boomtown Rats, it's that—'Look out for number one.' It sounds pretty selfish, but it's also very apropos of 1977. I want to rise above the common lot; I don't want

10

to be part of the huge lumpen masses who appear to be cloned from one mind. That's all we're saying, 'be yourself.' I'm not going to pretend to espouse some vague socialistic philosophy. I've been through that already."

—Bob Geldof, Boomtown Rats, 1977

"The main reason I'm dangerous is because I'm not afraid to say how I feel. I'm not afraid to say that I think Band Aid was diabolical. Or to say that I think Bob Geldof is a nauseating character. Many people find that very unsettling, but I'll say it as loud as anyone wants me to. In the first instance the record itself was absolutely tuneless. One can have great concern for the people of Ethiopia, but it's another thing to inflict daily torture on the people of England."

—Morrissey, 1985

WE LOVE THE WAY PUCCINI LAYS DOWN A TUNE
(CLASSICAL MUSIC)

"All the good music has already been written by people with wigs and stuff."

—Frank Zappa

"Beethoven I used to really like, and a guy called Handel wrote finger exercises that amazed me."

—Suzi Quatro, 1974

"I like Beethoven, especially the poems."

—Ringo Starr, 1964

"I think it was Segovia who said—hang on, is he still alive? well, if he is, he said it when he was pretty ill—'I'm still learning.' Which is the same for me."

—David Coverdale, Whitesnake, 1982

"I don't know many people who put on Tchaikovsky and go ape-shit."

—Pete Townshend, 1980

"People tell me they listen to classical music and I say 'Why?' Like, it just confuses and bothers me."

—Taime Downe, Faster Pussycat, 1987

11

"I'm keen to use cellos."

—Richard Butler, Psychedelic Furs, 1982

"I'm just as good a singer as Caruso...Have you ever heard me sing?"

—Bob Dylan, 1965

"I tell you, you stop smoking those cigarettes and you'll be able to sing like Caruso."

—Bob Dylan, 1969

"Y'know, I could sing like Caruso if I wanted to...but he's already done it."

—Tom Waits, 1988

"Copeland heard my arrangement of 'Hoedown' and he was knocked out by it. The only thing he said was why hadn't I played the triplets in a certain bar. We'd altered it with a very finely dotted quaver because it didn't swing the other way."

—Keith Emerson, ELP, 1977

"In the future we will have pop song cycles like classical Lieder, but we will create our own words, music, and orchestrations, because we are a generation of whole people."

—Judy Collins, 1968

"I made 'Bo Diddley' in '55, they started playing it, and everybody freaked out. Caucasian kids threw Beethoven into the garbage can."

—Bo Diddley, 1988

"The chord progression in the 'Highway Star' solo—Bm, to a Db, to a C, to a G—is a Bach progression."

—Ritchie Blackmore, Deep Purple, 1973

"You see, Bach had different periods. He went through writing things that could be very simplistic and things that were totally off the wall. For instance, the king calls him up and says, 'Hey! I'm having a party Saturday night, can you write me something?' Johann would say, 'All right, I'll bring down the boys and we'll do it.' That's how he wrote the simpler things, the dance numbers...Then Bach married his cousin, was kicked out of his family, had 25 kids, and went blind. He was really cool, I really liked him."

—Yngwie Malmsteen, 1985

MY NAME IS ROB, I GOT A REAL FUNKY CONCEPT

"I'm working on a project the logistics of which truly terrify me, and it would be premature to talk about it at the moment. It's something involving me as a performer."

—Robert Fripp, 1981

"*Tical 2000: Judgement Day* is my second LP, right? T2. That's Tical Tical. Two thousand is two words that begin with T. T.T. You got Method Man—M.M. Millennium starts and ends with M. M.M. M is also one thousand in Roman numerals; two of them make two thousand. I'm just perfect with this LP right now. My second LP, two thousand. The millennium is approaching, too, that's even better, man. People *need* this album right now."

—Method Man, Wu-Tang Clan, 1998

"*Supernature* is a story of good and evil. What I want to say to people is to leave each thing in its proper place, otherwise the monsters will be coming. Actually, the monsters exist within ourselves."

—Cerrone, 1978

"Quite frankly, I'm bored with making rock records, at least normal ones. I want the next Deep Purple album to have a concept about it, albeit a loose one. It's about time we made our *Sgt. Pepper*."

—Ian Gillian, Deep Purple, 2000

"It's a whole new sound, a whole new concept...It has no instruments, no keyboards, no guitars, just vocals and drum machines. No notes, no chords, no key—therefore, I don't have to sing in key because there's no key to sing in. You'll see, it's a whole new concept."

—Alan Vega, Suicide, 1988

"The premise behind Oingo Boingo is to remain in a state of motion, bouncing—boinging along, if you will—and to try to present something that is fun and entertaining but also has a point of view. Probably the most prevalent message connecting all three albums has been: question, resist, challenge."

—Danny Elfman, Oingo Boingo, 1983

"The first track is called 'I Wanna Live,' and the last line of 'Worm Man,' the last song, is 'I wish I was dead.' I guess it's a real conceptual album!"

—Joey Ramone, 1987

"We were going to write a song called 'I Love Rock and Roll About Rock and Roll,' but we thought that would be getting too weird."

—David Lowery, Camper Van Beethoven, 1987

"Gwar was created by the master of creation, an ambiguous being named Larry, as the ultimate doomsday device."

—Oderous Urungus, Gwar, 1990

"Sylvester Stallone heard our second album, *Premonition*, and really responded to the concept behind the band. So when he gave us the video of *Rocky III*, it seemed to us that everything Rocky was standing for was something the band was standing for—the basic American work ethic. We got to say a lot of things we'd been wanting to say for a long time."

—Jim Peterik, Survivor, 1982

"People are still talking about me as a guitarist, and I want recognition as a writer (I've written songs *and* magazine articles), as a designer of guitars, of sweaters, and of structural concepts."

—Rick Nielsen, Cheap Trick, 1979

"The thing that gets me about the 'Bad Touch' video is that no one ever mentions the midget. Everyone goes on about the gay guys being attacked, but the midget gets knocked over by a car and killed. And no one cares! At least the gay guy gets to live."

—Jimmy Pop, Bloodhound Gang, 2000

"I always knew if I was going to have a band, we were going to look flashy. Entertainment with your music—what a concept!"

—Marty Stuart, 1994

"A bit of Elvis, a bit of Bolan, a bit of dub, a bit of rap, zap it through a satellite dish and away we go!"

—Tony James, Sigue Sigue Sputnik, 1985

"Everybody's got a different musical note. Everybody gives off a certain musical note. What am I? I think I'm F-sharp. The thing is if you can go around and you meet somebody who's in F-sharp, you're in harmony, see. But if you meet somebody who's in F, it's a discord: you don't get on. The wind is in chords."

—Donovan, 1970

"'Barbie' was just a way into Aqua, and we've proved that."

—Soren Rasted, Aqua, 1998

"Disney thought I bastardized 'Heigh-Ho.' I think there should be a Heigh-Ho ride in Disneyland where they just pick these people up in their shorts and put 'em to work for eight hours."

—Tom Waits, 1988

GONNA BUY FIVE COPIES FOR MY MOTHER
(CRITICS)

"The critics seem to be giving us credit for depths to which we haven't yet sunk."

—Lol Crème, 10cc, 1974

"Them lot, I think they fancy me. I think they're all gay."

—Liam Gallagher on the British press, 1997

"I'll tell you, though, of all the people who have come to interview us, there isn't one I would consider spending the night with!"

—Patti Smith, 1978

"The critics come to our show and we provide them with a set list, and they stay for two songs and then go home and write their reviews. Some of the points they make are valid, but they just kill us after two songs. I once critiqued our critics in a song I wrote...it had a line that went, 'The critic is a legless running teacher.' Point closed."

—Bobby Kimball, Toto, 1983

"The only person who knows anything about my music is me."
—Prince

CREEM: Is that your notebook?
TOM WAITS: Yeah. Phone numbers. Grocery lists. You've got one. So do I.
—1988

"The only thing that bugs me is critics. It's like shooting at a flying saucer as it tries to land, without giving the occupants a chance to identity themselves."
—Jimi Hendrix

"I inherited a column called 'Sound Mix' in the *Los Angeles Reader* and soon found I was digging myself into the horribleness of rock 'n' roll writing. I would write about marginal groups that never sold any records. I would review a band called Grandpa Becomes a Fungus and then go to their little dungeon the following weekend, and it was the same five people as the week before, cowering while the ceiling leaked on them."
—Matt Groening, "The Simpsons," 1993

"Rock journalism is people who can't write interviewing people who can't talk for people who can't read."
—Frank Zappa

"We could lose it all by our fourth record. Then you'd say, 'Same old Dinosaur. I like their early stuff better.' And critics would say, 'Another tired offering from Dinosaur.' I can see that happening. But we'll keep on doing it because we've got nothing else to do."
—Lou Barlow, Dinosaur Jr, 1987

"*The National Enquirer* is the only paper I use for more than rolling joints."
—David Lee Roth, 1981

"If you give me a bad write-up, you dead."

—Jerry Lee Lewis, 1987

"But even poor Angus has to take stick a lot of times. Like there was one critic who said, 'Angus Young may be able to play a fucking fantastic solo. But can he do it on an acoustic guitar?' We couldn't fooking believe it! A lot of people who come to the shows are critics who are going to see *My Fair Lady* or Santana or Genesis. What do *they* know?"

—Brian Johnson, AC/DC, 1982

"Rock criticism is the easiest to write because it requires no skill at all! I mean, people who could not hope to survive in any other field of writing can be well-salaried in rock criticism, and they don't have to know anything about music, they only have to know about their own lifestyle."

—Todd Rundgren, 1979

"It's easy to sit behind a typewriter and criticize other people's efforts while you're sipping brandy."

—John Lydon, 1980

"There's no point listening to the music press, they're just middle class people with pens."

—Steve Mason, Beta Band, 1999

"We're gonna do our own rock opera. It's called *Albert*, and it's about a deaf, dumb, and blind boy who wants to play music but can't—so he becomes a rock critic."

—Jo Paul Jo, Dread Zeppelin, 1990

"We're not trying to sound heavy metal. It's just that metal kids have filtered in, and they seem to get it way more than *Village Voice* critics, who just kinda stand there."

—Rod Zombie, White Zombie, 1988

"Journalists from university killed pop music, now we're bringing it back. With 4,000,000 people unemployed, we need to be cheered up."

—Pete Waterman, Stock/Aitken/Waterman, 1987

"I could never figure out how we'd get a small corner in *Rolling Stone*'s encyclopedia while Lou Reed rates a whole page."
—Chris Squire, Yes, 1988

"You know that I basically like you in spite of myself. Common sense leads me to believe that you're an idiot, but somehow the epistemological things that you come out with sometimes betray the fact that you're kind of onomatopoetic in a subterranean reptilian way."
—Lou Reed to Lester Bangs, 1975

"Robert Hilburn wrote a good review of us in the *L.A. Times*, and I was really happy. Then I read Chuck Eddy's review of us in *Spin*—he compared us to the Dead Milkmen in a 'battle of the lame'; they won 'cause they had a hit single, and I was pissed off. But he did say one interesting thing, that I sing like that guy in 'Alf.' I dunno, I'd never watched 'Alf,' so I checked it out and he was right! I sound exactly like the guy in 'Alf.' So in some ways you have to hand it to Chuck Eddy—he can be a very perceptive critic."
—Bob Forrest, Thelonious Monster, 1987

"John Rockwell's a shithead. Nobody should read the *New York Times*."
—Johnny Ramone, 1980

"Byron Coley's just a loser, a third-rate writer, and I just don't give a fuck. It's kind of funny, because we have all these mutual friends, and they're saying, 'What is this with him? What's this about cocaine?! Did you fuck his wife or something?!' I don't know, probably not...I doubt it...not to the best of my knowledge."
—Peter Buck, R.E.M, 1987

"I can't believe you're from *Creem*. You're so *normal*. You remind me of my cousin back home—no offense—he's a mailman."
—Cheetah Chrome, Dead Boys, 1979

"Bob Greene from the *Chicago Sun-Times* came in with an attitude that we were sleazy. He wasn't exactly Mr. America."
—Sandy West, Runaways, 1977

"The reason why so many critics dislike Van Halen and like Elvis Costello so much is because they all *look* like Elvis Costello."

—David Lee Roth, 1980

"I've tried to say this for years now—in *no way* am I connected with a bunch of French lazy-arse intellectuals sitting on the West bank pontificating. These authors who have written books about me and the days I was in the Sex Pistols have an agenda before they write their book. They tried to fit me into their agenda. The language these guys use is absolutely despicable."

—John Lydon, 1994

WE DANCE JUST AS GOOD AS WE WANT

"God bless Zsa Zsa Gabor. She was the spark that lit the fire that flamed 'The Twist' on an international level."

—Chubby Checker, 1988

FLORIAN SCHNEIDER: We also kind of dance when we perform. It's not that we actually move our bodies, but it's this awareness of your whole body. You feel like a dancer.

RALF HUTTER: Your brain is dancing. The electronics are dancing around in the speakers.

—Kraftwerk, 1975

"I don't see myself doing silly little dance steps in 10 years, but I think the fact that I'm pretty immobile on stage is in my favour."

— Robert Smith, the Cure, 1986

DICK CLARK: Hello up there, Johnny, you all right? Feeling okay?

JOHN LYDON: Yeah, I'm all right.

CLARK: Would you like the audience up here or in their seats?

LYDON: No, they're welcome up here. Tell everyone to come on up and dance.

CLARK: Okay, they can all come, everybody out! One more time, here is Public Image Ltd.!"

—"American Bandstand," 1980

· LIFE TODAY: You know what I can't understand is how you keep that leg shaking at just right the tempo all the time you're singing.

ELVIS PRESLEY: Well, it gets hard sometimes. I have to stop and rest it—but it just automatically wiggles like that.

—1955

"I don't believe in A-D-E or any of that, and contrary to popular belief, you *cannot* dance to rock 'n' roll."

—John Lydon, 1981

"Dancing...I don't really do it that often, you know. I'm not very good at it, actually."

—Nick Cave, 1994

PARKING CARS AND PUMPING GAS
(DAY JOBS)

"My first job? Throwing live turkeys over a fifteen-foot electric fence. Few survived."

—Robyn Hitchcock, 1998

"I started watching this financial show in 1993. I started out with mutual funds, but then I wanted to get involved in the stock market. So I started reading up on stuff, watching these financial shows, and really getting into it. Actually, you get obsessed. I hate to say this, but I found it more exciting than rock 'n' roll at times. Because rock 'n' roll is pretty dull and these analysts are like the new rock 'n' roll stars."

—Joey Ramone, 1999

"I was washing dishes at the Greyhound bus station at the time. I couldn't talk back to my boss man. He would bring all these pots back for me to wash, and one day I said, 'I've got to do something to stop this man bringing back all these pots to me to wash,' and I said, 'Awap bob a lup bop a wop bam boom, take 'em out!'"

—Little Richard, 1969

"It's literally like Handsome Dick said on the first 'Tators record—this is just a hobby for us."

—Gregg Turner, math teacher and Angry Samoan, 1987

"There were some crazy things that happened on the set of 'The Mickey Mouse Club.' People were always telling jokes, playing pranks and stuff like that, but...I have to keep certain things secret."
—Christina Aguilera, 1999

"I was never dedicated to this band, I just figured I had nothing better to do. I had a complete Bo Diddley attitude towards the whole damn thing: may as well do this, because what else am I gonna do, go work?"
—Jeffrey Lee Pierce, the Gun Club, 1981

"I'm very involved with the salmon industry now, and in certain areas I am better known as a salmon farmer than I am as a musician— there are a couple of television programs in Britain in the next month, not about Ian Anderson as a musician but about Ian Anderson as a salmon farmer."
—Ian Anderson, Jethro Tull, 1988

"Here's how not to plan a career: a) split up with girlfriend; b) junk college; c) go to work in record shop; d) stay in record shops for rest of life."
—Nick Hornby, *High Fidelity*, 1995

"We'd rather, like, *do* music than follow it. If we gotta follow something, then we follow something that we don't really do, like films. And as soon as we start making our own movies, I don't think we're gonna go see anyone else's."
—MCA, Beastie Boys, 1986

"I could've been a painter, a cartoonist, a poet—I'm good at all those things. I can write brilliantly...I won essay competitions at school."
—Eddie Tudor-Pole, Ienpole Iudor, 1983

HAIL SATAN!
(THE DEVIL)

"Well, you know, people describe us sometimes as if we ran around fields with pitchforks in our hands. I think they expected flames to shoot out of the cover of our second album. Want some Doritos?"
—Ozzy Osbourne, 1971

"I don't want people to misconceive me as a spokesperson for the Church of Satan."
—Marilyn Manson

"Skinny Puppy is my way of expelling those demons from my soul."
—cEVIN Key, Skinny Puppy, 1985

"I've been Syd Barrett, lying in my sleeping bag in the recording studio. I was seeing the fucking demons."
—Richard Ashcroft, the Verve, 1997

"I noticed that on the last album, *Hell Awaits*, most of the songs were about Satan and hell, whereas on *Reign in Blood*, the main themes are murder, blood, and dismemberment. Was this a conscious shift of lyrical focus?"
—Alastair Sutherland (*Graffiti*), interviewing Slayer, 1987

"They are tools of the devil. Someone is behind them pulling their strings. I'm very afraid of those boys."
—Marilyn Manson on Hanson

"I was just lying in bed one night and woke up suddenly, and there was this black shape standing at the foot of me bed. I wasn't on drugs or anything, but for some reason I thought it was the Devil himself. It was almost as if this thing was saying to me, 'It's time to either pledge allegiance or piss off.'"
—Geezer Butler, Black Sabbath, 1997

"We're off to introduce the world to the ways of Lucifer. If the world hasn't ended by next year then we'll continue to make it until the end of time."
—Marilyn Manson, 1997

STUDIO 54, WHERE ARE YOU?
(DISCO)

"Apparently they can dance to *Disco Party*. I don't have the physical equipment to do it, but as a musician I'm led into the right grooves."

—Percy Faith, 1976

"God had to create disco music so that I could be born and be successful. I was blessed. I am blessed."

—Donna Summer, 1979

"After we recorded 'Jive Talkin' everybody said it was disco. We didn't even know what disco was at the time."

—Barry Gibb, Bee Gees, 1976

"I'm glad to see the Clash have gone disco. It's about time they made some money."

—David Lee Roth, 1981

"Sex disco music will be fabulous. I want to have someone fuck on the record and record it, the sounds. Not moaning or groaning, but the sounds of sex, the sounds of touching, the actual sounds of penetration. Nice music and close miking. It's not gonna be a record for sex, it's a record for dancing, with sex."

—Sylvester, 1978

"Disco is like a great porno film. If the characters and filming techniques are interesting, it's great for five minutes. That's what disco music is, good for five minutes. All the audience is interested is in tapping their feet. If that's all you want to hear, fantastic, but it bores the shit out of me."

—Herbie Mann, 1976

"Listen, I would have tried to kill disco if it didn't die by itself."

—Jim McDonnell, Stray Cats, 1983

"I used to go clubbing a lot in the early '70s in New York, when disco happened...I gave Rod Stewart a popper at Studio 54 one night. I was going, 'Come on dear, have a dance.' She was, 'I don't dance, dear.'"

—Elton John, 2001

"I know it sounds funny. During the recording of 'Love to Love You Baby,' I had much more romantic thoughts than the record led you to believe."

—Donna Summer, 1979

"The few times I wrote songs with emphasis on the lyrics, the record company told me to stop it because the words just interfered."

—Cerrone, 1979

"I think that a lifetime of listening to disco music is a high price to pay for one's sexual preference."

—Quentin Crisp

"Maybe I don't know the 'in' clubs to visit, but every disco I've been to is full of pimps, hookers, and dealers."

—Herbie Mann, 1976

"The disco craze is definitely a fad. I'm doing something brand new next year."

—Monti Rock III, a.k.a. Disco Tex, 1976

DON'T PICK FIGHTS WITH THE BULLIES OR THE CADS
(DISSING)

"I hate R.E.M. They're popular, is that a good reason?"
—Michael Gerald/Bill Hobson/Dan Hobson, Killdozer, 1988

"There's too much written in minor keys. We call those bands 'A Flock of Crying Babies.'"

—Ivan Doroschuk, Men Without Hats, 1983

"Pete Townshend's gotten to the point that he waits until the photographers are well-aimed before he leaps. He's not very spontaneous."

—Ritchie Blackmore, Deep Purple, 1973

"Worst album I ever heard 'cept for my parts. Johnny Cash is the worst singer in the world. Roy Orbison is the ugliest sonofabitch I ever seen. Carl Perkins is a one-hit wonder."

—Jerry Lee Lewis on the *Class of '55* reunion album

"I like watching public downfalls. David Bowie: when he came, everybody thought he was from Mars, but then you realize he's just this businessman. Bowie a hero? Oh no, I hate him—useless rubbish."

—Ian Brown, Stone Roses, 1990

"Nobody's gonna take any notice because it's a heavy metal album. It has to be by Paul bloody Weller or Pete Shelley. It's ridiculous! What have they ever done? Nothing! Just because they were in the college debating society, they're supposed to have a better view of the world than I have? What have they ever done? Nothing! They have no idea."

—Lemmy, Motorhead, 1986

"I don't know, there are a lot of horrible bands. Take Hüsker Dü. They're all right, y'know, but they ain't doing anything that we didn't already do...and besides, they don't look so good."

—Joey Ramone, 1986

"That's the problem with crap like Paul Weller and the Style Council...He takes influences like Smokey and the Isleys and comes out sounding all sugary. Not only does it sound like two little pigs with very high-pitched voices, it sounds like clichéd pigs."

—Mick Hucknall, Simply Red, 1986

"A kid in England on the dole cannot relate to Wham!"

—Johnny Marr, the Smiths, 1987

"When you listen to Bon Jovi, you can hear corruption. You can hear money changing hands."

—Ben Vaughn, 1988

"I think Madonna is particularly revolting. I find it hard to imagine why anyone would want to so cheapen themselves. The things she says are disgusting, and I'd kill anyone who used her kind of language around me."
—Whitney Houston, 1988

"You don't want to get too close to Madonna, you know what I mean?"

—Robert Plant, 1993

"Obviously Madonna reinforces everything absurd and offensive. Desperate womanhood. Madonna is closer to organized prostitution than anything else. I mean, the music industry is obviously prostitution anyway, but there are degrees. For me Prince conveys nothing. The fact that he's successful in America is interesting simply because he's mildly fey and that hasn't happened before there. Boy George, again I think he really doesn't say anything either."

—Morrissey, 1986

"Classic Van Halen made you want to drink, dance, and fuck. Current Van Halen encourages us to drink milk, drive a Nissan, and have a relationship."

—David Lee Roth

"Let's see in five years which of us is still making records and which of us is sucking dicks in the bus depot for change."

—Steve Albini on Urge Overkill, 1993

"Mick Jagger is a scared little boy who is about as sexy as a pissing toad."

—Truman Capote

"Go play with the other boys. Don't bother me. Go play with the Rolling Wings."

—John Lennon, 1980

"What better example of 'cynical pop strategism,' if that's the right word, is there than the whole 'The Rattle and the Hum' marketing exercise?"

—Neil Tennant, Pet Shop Boys, 1988

"There's always the moment when I insist on toning down something horrible I've said about U2."

—Neil Tennant, Pet Shop Boys, 1994

"Would we shag Liam? No way, I think he's repulsive, and I'd like to smack him in the mouth. I think Noel's cool. He keeps himself to himself, but Liam? Oh no."

—Posh Spice, 1997

"Why aren't people on the cases of the real assholes of this world, like Axl Rose and Steve Albini, both of whom should be exterminated. Really, they should leave on a shuttle to the sun. They shouldn't be on the earth. Because they're not good for anything."

—Courtney Love, 1994

"If my music ever got as laid-back and mellow as Eric Clapton's, I'd pack it in. Or shoot myself."

—Paul Weller, 1995

"The Rock and Roll Hall of Fame means no royalty checks. I was indicted, I mean inducted, into the Rock and Roll Hall of Fame by threat. I told Chuck Berry I'd kill him. I killed Elvis Presley anyway—got rid of him, finally. It took a long time. I got him! I got rid of Ricky Nelson. Everybody around me dies."

—Jerry Lee Lewis, 1987

"One would hear more vocal passion from an ape under anaesthetic. Inexcusably dim."

—Morrissey reviews Bucks Fizz's "Golden Days," 1985

"You've got a pool of young minds—clean water—and you drop in Camper Van Beethoven. In my mind, that's pissing in the gene pool.

—Henry Rollins, 1988

"In 10 years, people will say we were the first real crossover band. I would like to have some good grades in Sweden. For the last album the reviewers all wanted to throw up; it was like wet spaghetti in your face. Maybe we should have lyrics that nobody understands, like R.E.M."

—Jonas Berggren, Ace of Base, 1995

"Bryan Ferry. Jesus. He was cute for awhile."

—Lou Reed, 1975

"I saw Dylan in New York seven, eight months ago. We don't have a lot to talk about. We're not great friends. Actually, I think he hates me."

—David Bowie, 1976

"I'm pretty sure that Pearl Jam didn't go out of their way to challenge their audience as much as we did with the record. They're a safe rock band. They're a pleasant rock band that everybody likes. God, I've had much better quotes in my head about this."

—Kurt Cobain, Nirvana, 1994

CHRIS LOWE: I don't suppose Prince has bothered to come. He's just a tragic rock 'n' roller.

NEIL TENNANT: He's probably gone to see the Scorpions. Let's face it, he doesn't sell as many records as Axl Rose, our number one fan.

—Pet Shop Boys, 1993

"I've always had incredible amounts of self-confidence. It's based not on how good we are, but on how bad most other people are."

—Robert Smith, the Cure, 1995

"Beatles, eh? Oh yes. I seem to remember their off-key caterwauling on the old Sullivan show."

—Montgomery Burns, "The Simpsons," 1991

A HOOKAH-SMOKING CATERPILLAR HAS GIVEN US THE CALL
(DRUGS)

"Me father give me herb when I was young. He'd say, 'Ziggy, take a draw.'"

—Ziggy Marley, 1989

"There were sound musicological reasons why psychedelic music happened. Rather than being some drug-induced thing, it was really a bunch of serious folkie musicologists who played blues and bluegrass joining forces with guys who played at the edge of town, chewed gum, and couldn't put two sentences together—the rock and roll players."

—Barry Melton, Country Joe and the Fish, 1997

"I'm only being refreshingly honest when I say I'd like my drugs delivered to me onstage by bow-tied dwarfs on a silver platter."

—Wayne Hussey, the Mission, 1987

"He wanted to be an example to young people. People say that, because later on it was found that he had used drugs, that therefore he could not be a good example. They overlook the fact he never used illegal drugs. It was always drugs prescribed by his physician."
—Richard Nixon on Elvis Presley

"Grass is the same emotional blocker as alcohol or cocaine. It just takes you off into another land. For years, I quite liked that land; in fact I loved that land!"
—Ringo Starr, 1992

"I think *Electric Music* is the best psychedelic record ever made. Millions of people have tripped to that album. It's guaranteed!"
—Country Joe McDonald, 1997

"Everything is better when you're straight, except fucking up."
—Deborah Harry, Blondie, 1979

"The only thing pop music has ever succeeded in persuading people to do is take drugs."
—Neil Tennant, Pet Shop Boys, 1991

"Pink Floyd is the best music to listen to when one is stoned on marijuana. Of course, I never inhaled."
—Salman Rushdie

"I loved the Sex Pistols, especially John Lydon. I didn't really know them, although I shared the same drug dealer as Sid Vicious."
—Marianne Faithfull, 1994

"I'm too devoted to my art to fall foul of drugs."
—Whitney Houston, 1988

"The press don't know me at all. They haven't had a chance to sit down and talk with the real Bobby Brown. Rumours of drug abuse: that's all bullshit. Alcohol abuse: that's bullshit too. I went to the Betty Ford Center for my mind."
—Bobby Brown, 1996

"I've only flipped out once or twice. I was in a club in London and there were like, big holes, big pits on the floor. Pits of fire! It was weird, man. I had to step around them and over them and stuff. And it was all red like the devil's den, and there were devils blocking the toilet. I didn't go, obviously."

—Wayne Hussey, the Mission, 1987

HOW WONDERFUL LIFE IS WHILE I'M IN THE WORLD
(EGO)

TOM SNYDER: It's unfortunate that we're all out of step except you. I wish something could be done about that.

JOHN LYDON: This is what I've been telling the world for about five, six years now. I wish you'd all grow up.

—"Tomorrow Show," 1980

"I got guys walking up on stage, grabbing hold of me and saying, 'Hey boy, you're gonna be great.'"

—Leo Sayer, 1974

"Of course, I do occasionally arouse primeval instincts, but I mean, most men can do that. They can't do it to so many. I just happen to be able to do it to several thousand people. It's fun to do that."

—Mick Jagger

"We are a bit holier than most groups, when you think about it. We've got a lot more going for us. In fact, we've always been the classiest band, I think. There's intelligence, self-parody...just about everything you could possibly want. Overall greatness is how I'd put it."

—Ian McCulloch, Echo and the Bunnymen, 1984

"I couldn't live without television! Occasionally the great god is switched on...I watched things like Muhammad Ali. Now, next to me, I think he's got to be the most fantastic character."

—Robert Plant, 1974

"We're the first honest band to hit this planet in about two thousand million years."

—Johnny Rotten, 1976

"I just recommend people get out and buy the video. It's important for a couple of reasons. And they are this: There are a lot of people who in their life are never ever going to get the chance to see Manowar live. Ever."

—Joey Demaio, 2000

"All that journalists had to write about the last six years were Duran Duran, Wham!, Culture Club, and all these safe groups who really had nothing to say for themselves. And then along came Sigue Sigue Sputnik, saying this is the new attitude, the new approach."

—Martin Degville, Sigue Sigue Sputnik, 1986

"You would never think it, but people's major important events and landmarks are associated with us."

—Felipe, the Village People, 1988

"Musically, we are more talented than any Bob Dylan. Musically, we are more talented than Paul McCartney. Mick Jagger, his lines are not clear. He doesn't know how he should produce a sound. I'm the new modern rock and roll. I'm the new Elvis."

—Rob Pilatus, Milli Vanilli, 1989

"I happen to believe I'm a genius. As time proves me right, I'm becoming less and less afraid to say so."

—Terence Trent D'Arby, 1988

"The Beatles don't exist any more and I was going five years before the Beatles, so no one's ever going to catch me up. I'll always be ahead of everybody."

—Cliff Richard, 1992

31

"I am blessed with a terrific voice. It's a God-given thing."

—Roy Orbison, 1988

"Anybody's first two albums against my first two albums, I'm there. I'm with the Beatles."

—Noel Gallagher, Oasis, 1996

"I am of a mood these days that tells me that I'm a right-wing fascist liberal. I cover all bases. I'm very legitimate on a number of levels. That's why I'm still here. That's why I still matter. I'm the only honest commodity around. I always was. I mean, even when I was an asshole, I was an asshole on my own terms."

—Lou Reed, 1978

"You may hear a lot of stories from other bands about Manowar because naturally they are jealous. I would be if I were them too. Come on, think about it."

—Joey Demaio, 2000

"None of the new generation can ever be the Godfather. The only people that qualify are myself and Sinatra. It's God's business that nobody can fill my shoes."

—James Brown, 1988

"Look at Africa and Iceland: they have nothing in common except Ace of Base."

—Ulf 'Buddha' Ekberg, Ace of Base, 1995

"I don't like the way my teeth protrude. I'm going to have them done, but I just haven't had the time. Apart from that…I'm perfect."

—Freddie Mercury

"It's quite sad, isn't it? We listen to ourselves almost exclusively."

—Simon Gilbert, Suede, 1997

"I'd hate to think I was a conventional snob. I have not forgotten my humble origins. But I would admit that Louis XIV is more up my alley than Karl Marx."

—Bryan Ferry, 1993

"I always was a good listener. Less so now. I talk more about myself now. I'm always waiting for someone to finish talking so that I can go, 'Oh yeah, me, I did this and this...'"

—Randy Newman, 1988

"It's strange we're not seen as credible. We should be. People ask why we make commercial pop music. Look at Nirvana, they've sold a lot, they're a commercial band with classic pop arrangements. They're more dirty than us, that's all."

—Jonas Berggren, Ace of Base, 1995

"'You Trip Me Up' is pure summer. It should be number one for about forty-two weeks, and then we'll take it to the United States of America and then it'll be number one there."

—Jim Reid, Jesus and Mary Chain, 1985

"I can be something of a tyrant in a working situation. Well, in a living situation, too."

—Madonna, 1991

"Y'know, son, there's only been four of us: Al Jolson, Jimmie Rodgers, Hank Williams, and Jerry Lee Lewis. That's your only four fuckin' stylists that ever lived. We could write, sing, yodel, dance, fuck, or what—makes no damn difference. The rest of these idiots is either ridin' a fuckin' horse, pickin' a guitar, or shootin' somebody in some stupid damn movie."

—Jerry Lee Lewis, 1979

"Have you ever heard David Crosby warm up for a show? 'Me, me, me, me, me, me, me.' "

—Graham Nash, 2000

MADAM ONASSIS GOT NOTHIN' ON YOU
(FAME)

"I have four boxes of Kraft macaroni and cheese in my house now. I really live a glamorous lifestyle."

—Chris Robinson, Black Crowes, 1995

"I accompanied Madonna to the Grammys this year. She just called me up and asked if I wanted to go with her...it's cool that she likes me enough to ask me to go with her. I wasn't nervous—meeting stars like that doesn't bother me. Did she come on to me? No, man! Ha! It wasn't like that!"

—Lil' Bow Wow, 2001

"Look, here's a picture of me and Madonna. We're backstage in Jesus and Mary Chain's dressing room. I'm shirtless and she's whispering in my ear, 'Look—who are they, taking my picture?' The only words she ever said to me. What a woman."

—Gibby Haynes, the Butthole Surfers, 1987

"I actually passed Madonna one evening coming out of a studio. I was dressed like a nut, a bag lady. I said hello to her, but I don't think she recognized me. She seemed kind of alone, with all her bodyguards. I hailed a cab and went home where the light was on, and my husband and cats were waiting for me."

—Cyndi Lauper, 1994

"I won't be happy until I'm as famous as God."

—Madonna

"I can walk anywhere and no one cares. Also, I'm always changing my hair, so that helps."

—Lindsey Buckingham, Fleetwood Mac, 1982

"I realized I was really a rock star when I started getting paternity suits from places I'd never been. I showed them to other rock groups, who said, 'Oh yeah, you got one from the Carlisles in Ohio too, how about that!"

—Mickey Dolenz, Monkees, 1986

"When you're bounding across the States in a bus at about 90 miles per hour and someone comes up and says the album's number one in America, you just say, 'Oh, that's good,' and then you stare rather blankly out of the window for a while."

—Colin Hay, Men at Work, 1983

"When 'Blue Velvet' was number one, I went to Vegas. I went to the health club, and Dean Martin was there. He was one of my idols. I said, 'Dean, I'm Bobby Vinton and I have the number one record in America, "Blue Velvet."' He said, 'Never heard of it, and I don't know you.' I said, 'I just came in first in a big singing poll. Frank

Sinatra came in second, and Elvis Presley third.' Frank was getting a rubdown next to Dean, and he didn't know me either. They cared about Bobby Vinton about as much as I care about the guy who has a number one today."

—Bobby Vinton, 1988

"I'm in a situation where I couldn't even go into a drugstore and get a hamburger."

—Joe Strummer, the Clash, 1979

"We just can't be seen in public. What's to keep some guy whose girlfriend has been playing BTO records all the time from breaking both my legs if he sees me on the street?"

—Randy Bachman, 1975

"Of course, we weren't always superstars, there was a time when we were ordinary commoners just like you."

—Ian Hunter, *Mott the Hoople Live*, 1974

"Being a cult figure is a polite word for being a loser."

—Adam Ant, 1984

"People ask me if it's hard being me. I answer, 'To a degree, but it's not any more difficult than being George Michael.'"

—Bob Dylan, 1988

"The kids phone me up 24 hours a day. When I check into a hotel, I don't use an alias. I want to be me, Ozzy Osbourne. But it's tough because of my position in life. It's the price you pay for fame. The Pope is so famous that he must want to piss up a fuckin' wall."

—Ozzy Osbourne, 1984

"Man, I feel privileged...I met the drummer for ZZ Top. I met Eddie Money. I met Van Halen when they were little stuff, and I found the guitar player from Journey—who played with Carlos Santana—I found his ring where he'd left it at a white porcelain sink backstage at the Cotton Bowl. I met Arnold Palmer, Mickey Mantle. I met Pancho

Segura, and I tried to get him to sign my autograph and he said, 'Not now, son. Not now.' Don January, the famous golfer. His brother broke my mother's arm."

—Gibby Haynes, the Butthole Surfers, 1987

"I made a single, a version of the Shirelles' 'Will You Still Love Me Tomorrow' and I got up the courage to call record stores and try to sell it. I had a little speech prepared: 'Hi, I'm Moe Tucker from the Velvet Underground.'"

—Moe Tucker, 1993

I WISH I WAS YOUR MOTHER
(FAMILY)

"I came from a religious family. 'You'd better not be singing no devil's music!' But my first record was a hit, and when $800 came in everybody said 'A-men!'"

—Chuck Berry, 1986

"How could you possibly top 'The End'? What's left once you've fucked your mother and killed your father?"

—Robbie Krieger, the Doors, 1994

"The first tour I did with my own band was six weeks long. And I realized it was too long for everybody: my mother, my kids, and me. I had to wait till the youngest kids were a lot older before I could go on the road longer than a month. Nappies, bath time, picking up kids from school—it'll never sell...it just ain't rock 'n' roll."

—Moe Tucker, 1993

"My little sister really wanted a kite, but my mum said no, we already had enough stuff. My sister was really upset, so I took her to the park, tied string to me, and told her she could use me as a kite. I thought the experience would be good for me, too."

—Lisa Stansfield, 1990

"If I have a pelvic move in my show, I can't not do it just because my mother's there."

—L.L. Cool J, 1987

"Well, my mom admits we're doing well. But then she'll add in the same breath, 'Yep, and so's crack!"
—Paul Leary, the Butthole Surfers, 1989

"Bread and babies, as every housewife knows, is a full-time job."
—John Lennon, 1980

"The family itself is a vanishing artifact. In the '90s, if you have a family and the people inside the family have affection for one another, it's kind of a miracle. It's mutant behaviour."
—Frank Zappa, 1993

"I think structure at a very young age is imperative. It's like, Japan now has a square watermelon. It's much easier to store and you can slice it like bread. I think the same holds true for children. They should be bound tightly and learn to conform. Don't want 'em growing like a hedge."
—Tom Waits, 1988

"I've seen acts come and go; now most of them are pumping gas again. So there must be something to it besides a hit record. The Cowsills, they'll hang in there because they have the family thing going for them. People like that. They'll make Vegas. Ya know what I mean?"
—Phil Everly, 1968

EVERYTHING WE DO, WE DO IT FOR YOU
(FANS)

"I want to massage the audience to death."
—Marty Balin, Jefferson Starship, 1978

"Right now on this very tour we've got this husband and wife team who look almost like a completely normal couple from New York City. They have left their jobs to follow us all around America because they've been completely taken by Revillomania. They're totally obsessed."
—Fay Fife, the Revillos, 1981

"Rubber workers used to get off from the factories near us and come see us play."

—Gerald Casale, Devo, 1978

"One gets the impression that the average American rock fan must be mentally retarded. I've been told that L.A. is four years behind London and that New York is two years behind London. Why that is—or whether that's true—I don't know."

—Joe Jackson, 1979

"There are boys who want to marry me. I just write back to them and say, in the nicest possible way, 'I'm too young to get married and you're too young as well! You should concentrate on your schoolwork.'"

—Samantha Fox

"We're still fans ourselves. We sorta remember what it was like before we made it."

—Lemmy, Motorhead, 1981

"My dream of course is that our entire audience should be composed of people with their stupidly shaved heads."

—Peter Gabriel, 1974

"I have an obsession with teenage hysteria, and just to find *myself* at the centre of any of it I just find quite thrilling."

—Neil Tennant, Pet Shop Boys, 1989

"I'm not gonna apologize to anybody for *Metal Machine Music*, and I don't think any disclaimer shoulda been put on the cover. Just because some kid paid $7.98 for it, I don't care if they pay $59.98 or $75 for it, they should be GRATEFUL I put that fucking thing out, and if they don't like it they can go eat rat shit. I make records for me."

—Lou Reed, 1975

"I've decided there's a vast mass of people out there who have little or no interest in music, who've stopped buying records, and who could like the Fall. *They're* the people I'm trying to reach."

—Mark E. Smith, the Fall, 1981

"The audience were nodding their heads, so we thought, do the same, copy the audience. Heads down, nodding. The Quo stance was born."

—Rick Parfitt, Status Quo, 2001

"Speaking of sex, yesterday I got a good fan letter, it contained a bag of—oooooh, goody, a check for the fan club."

—Alice Cooper, 1972

"Yeah, well, I have a lot of fans. I don't have sex with them, though."

—Deborah Harry, Blondie, 1979

"Onstage, I make love to 25,000 people, then I go home alone."

—Janis Joplin

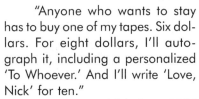

"Anyone who wants to stay has to buy one of my tapes. Six dollars. For eight dollars, I'll autograph it, including a personalized 'To Whoever.' And I'll write 'Love, Nick' for ten."

—Nick Cave, 1985

"As sweaty and as tired as we are, we're going to go over there and sign T-shirts for you, shake hands, and say 'What up?' You know why? There's only one reason we would do this. It's three words. We love you."

—Joseph Simmons, Run-D.M.C., 1998

"If they don't buy my records, they can bark my hole. And if they don't buy my albums, they can use my dick for a walkin' pole. God, that was awful. Erase that. Naw, I'll tell ya what I think of my fans. I think of them exactly the way they think about me."

—Jerry Lee Lewis, 1977

"The only people who say we look like girls are ones who've lost their girlfriends because they like our band!"

—Zac Hanson, 1998

"They are very young, these people that buy records in America. They may be intelligent, but they are unsophisticated."

—Mick Jagger, 1982

"This guy in swimming trunks, soaking wet because he was just in the pool, decides he was going to jump on top of me because he just loves the fucking band, but he was drunk out of his mind and his girlfriend was puking in the back. And even the owner of the restaurant figures that. I mean, this is Virginia Beach. And I said, 'Don't you think you should deal with your chick right now?!' And he's like, 'Rikki fuckin' Rockett Poison dude!!' And I'm like, 'Dude, your chick is pukin'. What if she dies? Go fuckin' deal with her.'"

—Ricki Rockett, Poison, 2000

REPORTER: Why do you think you get more fan mail than anyone else in the group?

RINGO STARR: I dunno. I suppose it's because more people write to me.

—1964

WE GET THE FUNNIEST LOOKS FROM EVERYONE WE MEET
(FASHION)

"He noticed my shoes, and then he really opened up. Andy Warhol loves my shoes!"

—David Bowie, 1972

"I think the higher the heel, the better the leg shape. I think there's been an unfortunate trend against this teetering around in the last few years. It's caused me a lot of grief. As I walk down the streets of our major cities and see only chunky boots, I shake my head sadly and think about what the world has come to."

—Bryan Ferry, 1993

"I mean, in a couple years' time I'll probably look at a picture of me in platforms and say, 'What the hell was I doing?'"

—Elton John, 1973

"I can spot a pair of flares a mile away—I hate 'em."

—John Lydon, 1981

"Just once I would like to persuade the audience not to wear any article of blue denim. If only they could see themselves in a pair of brown corduroys like mine instead of this awful, boring blue denim. If Jesus Christ came back today, He and I would get into our brown corduroys and go to the nearest jean store and overturn the racks of blue denim. Then we'd get crucified in the morning."

—Ian Anderson, Jethro Tull

"I don't like to look at groups who come out standing looking like they've just been drowning at Big Sur for five years. I could never go onstage in denims."

—Elton John, 1973

"Long hair is an unpardonable offense which should be punishable by death."

—Morrissey, 1986

"I remember when I was eleven years old I had a real short haircut like Elvis Costello's, and I used about a tube of Brylcreem a day. I was the only one in class who could do headstands, and I'd leave big grease spots on the cement. I was very proud of that haircut."

—David Lee Roth, 1981

"A lot of people think my hair's a hat."

—Patti LaBelle, 1986

"For the modern career girl, a wig is essential."

—Lady Miss Kier, Deee-Lite, 1991

"I used to feel that I dyed my hair red because what was in my brains at that time was red."

—Cyndi Lauper, 1986

"People just stop and look at me. The only time I've reacted the whole summer was checking into the hotel yesterday. There were two blokes, one pointing and one laughing. I actually had to walk up to them and ask why they were laughing. They went dead silent, put their heads down and said, 'We weren't laughing at you.' I just said, 'Why don't you have the courage of your fucking convictions? If you're gonna laugh, laugh.'"

—Robert Smith, the Cure, 1995

41

"The photographers were there and wanted Elton John and me to pose for pictures together, so I asked Elton if I could kiss him, but he didn't answer me so I didn't. Maybe he didn't hear me. He was wearing a hat because of his hair transplant."
—*The Andy Warhol Diaries*, 1977

"When we were given the opportunities by promoters and our own finances to do something beyond what we had been doing, then I sat down with my mask-maker and started doing some things."
—Peter Gabriel, 1974

"We're taking off the masks and showing our new robot skin."
—Thomas Bangalter,
Daft Punk, 2001

"Here's my original Clown mask. The only person I let wear it is my little boy. You can smell it if you want, though."
—Shawn Crahan,
Slipknot, 2000

"With beauty comes pain. My feet are hurting and this corset is very painful."
—Michelle Williams,
Destiny's Child, 2000

"I may wear black underwear now and again, but that's it."
—Angus Young, AC/DC, 1982

"You know what? I *did* wear a thong before! It was a long time ago, a deep dark secret in the closet that I never wanted anyone to know...It was a *male* thong, though."
—Sisqo, 2000

"You know who buys all of his stuff at Sears Roebuck? David Bowie!"
—Iggy Pop, 1980

"I feel safe in white because, deep down inside, I'm an angel."
—Puff Daddy, 2000

REPORTER: Do you like topless bathing suits?
RINGO: We've been wearing them for years.
—1964

"I put makeup on when I wake up. Sometimes, if I'm going shopping, depending upon what shop I'm going to, I wear it. If I'm going to the supermarket, I generally put it on. If I'm going 'round to the news agent's, I don't bother."
—Robert Smith, the Cure, 1987

"I remember thinking that with the four of us, Kraftwerk looked a bit like an odd string quartet. Concerning the clothes, it was basically the same: I had to wear a suit to perform classical contemporary things, and I also had to wear a suit with Kraftwerk!"
—Karl Bartos, Kraftwerk

"You have no idea how much it costs to look this cheap."
—Steven Tyler, Aerosmith

"I love kilts—they're really sexy. Unfortunately, they're so expensive they're fast becoming extinct among the common man. But now and again you go to a party and there's a bonny lad in a kilt with no knickers on—and honey, there's nothing better than sticking your hand up a kilt and feeling a naked bottom."
—Shirley Manson, Garbage, 1996

"For me the '60s were diabolical. I never knew what to put on. I was all alone because I dressed Ivy League, and I still do."
—Charlie Watts, 1996

"I know I look ridiculous sometimes, absolutely idiotic, but remember, when I started I was quite rotund."
—Elton John, 1976

"I think we're getting away from the glamour. Though we're not dying our hair jet black or anything. Now my hair's red. It's almost a strawberry blonde...there's a bit of blonde in there somewhere."
—Kenny MacLean, Platinum Blonde, 1986

"My accountant has to figure out how to deal with $600 worth of bandages a year. I like Boots brand, by the way."

—Nash the Slash

"I don't wear the school suit—the school suit wears *me*."

—Angus Young, AC/DC, 1995

"Somebody asks me, 'Dave, what's it mean when you say somebody's rocking or when somebody's not rocking?' I say, 'I'll illustrate: a guy with black socks, black shoes, blue and white Bermuda shorts, Hawaiian luau shirt, a Nikon and a jackknife around his neck, zinc oxide on his nose, a pair of sunglasses, a fishing hat with all the badges on it, and he's staring up at the tall buildings—that's rock 'n' roll.'"

—David Lee Roth, 1984

EVERY TIME I EAT VEGETABLES IT MAKES ME THINK OF YOU
(FOOD)

"I like it well done. Cooked. I ain't orderin' a pet."

—Elvis Presley on meat

"There are only forty people in the world and five of them are hamburgers."

—Captain Beefheart

"A song like 'Chicken of the Sea' is just a whole bunch of sexual puns—incorporating seafood."

—Mike Chandler, Raunch Hands, 1986

"My costume was so tight that I couldn't sit down in it. It was terrible, and I cursed myself for not slimming a bit before wearing that thing. And afterwards, of course, I went on the strictest diet you can imagine."

—Björn Ulvaeus, ABBA

"Bacon is dangerous 'cos your pig has no veins. And because pigs have no veins, they get bit by a rattlesnake and it don't affect 'em. And they walk roun' with all that poison inside of 'em. And when you eat your chop or your bacon it could still be fulla that shit."

—Bo Diddley, 1996

"I don't eat meat. Only bacon."

—Lisa Loeb, 2001

YOUR MIRROR'S GETTIN' JAMMED UP WITH ALL YOUR FRIENDS
(FRIENDSHIP)

"We're phone friends. We talk about how to record that drum sound on 'Ant Music' and stuff. He talks about my dancing and I talk about his dressing. Could you say 'Hi' to him for me?"

—Michael Jackson on Adam Ant, 1983

"First I beg him not to wear his sunglasses, and of course he complies, because I'm stronger than he is. Then we exchange powder puffs—we both powder our noses—and we compare bank accounts."

—Madonna on Michael Jackson, 1991

"The Pistols and the Clash used to come around a lot, and we're spiritual friends. We're all doing the same kinds of things...But I don't take any stick from those guys. I don't treat them with any respect at all because they're very rude. Which is unnecessary."

—Ian Dury, 1978

"We have as many friends as we have personalities. Do you know who said that? Emerson. Keith Emerson."

—Morrissey, 1995

THE GIRLS ARE ALL AROUND BUT NONE OF THEM WANNA GET WITH ME
(GIRLS)

"Sam Cooke was a beautiful cat, with everything going for him, and I can honestly say Sam loved women. Short ones, tall ones, fat ones, and blind ones, he would tell me that all of them have got something to offer."

—Bobby Womack

"I hope there's a very confused 14-year-old girl out there who will hear me speak or hear me sing and derive some sort of strength from that. I try to be a good representative of women.

45

Anyway, you can be sure you won't see any background vocalists in tight skirts in my band. If I need any they'll wear potato sacks and Birkenstocks."

—Alanis Morissette, 1999

"Some people seem to think I'm something of a Women's Lib symbol, because I'm a girl drummer. But to be quite honest, I've never really got into Women's Lib."

—Karen Carpenter, 1974

"I'm abso-fuckin'-total-lutely for women's liberation. The women who do secretly want to be dominated—and I know quite a few who do—have those attitudes because that's what they were taught."

—David Lee Roth, 1981

"I guess I am a feminist of sorts, I love women so much, and celebrate the female side in me because I appreciate it so much."

—Steven Tyler, Aerosmith, 1994

"It's not about being a woman, it's about being an attractive woman. It's true. And it's the same for males. Why do you think all the heavy metal guys go heavy on the big image look, that pretty boy look? I don't know, maybe the Beastie Boys are going to change that now."

—Stacey Q, 1987

"Madonna made it possible for me to be interpreted correctly. There's nothing I could do now that would be over the top. She's like the motorboat, and we're all water-skiing like the Go-Go's on the back of it."

—Liz Phair, 1994

"Once Lita, Sandy, and I threw a guy out of our hotel room in San Diego because he said, 'Girls can't rock 'n' roll!' Those were the last words he said."

—Cherie Currie, Runaways, 1977

"Women are more dolphin-like than men, and they're obviously better looking. Proboscis monkeys look pretty good too."

—Captain Beefheart, 1988

WOULD I WRITE A BOOK OR SHOULD I TAKE TO THE STAGE?
(GOALS AND ASPIRATIONS)

"Our goal was to have little 10-year-old boys slicking their hair back and growing tiny moustaches."

—Ron Mael, Sparks, 1983

"I was combing in the mirror and my mother saw me, and I said, 'I'm not going to school.' She said, 'Are you crazy? This is your last semester. You're so close to graduation.' I said, 'I'm going to Hollywood.' And that's what I did."

—Barry White, 1988

"How many Pet Shop Boys does it take to change a light bulb? Two. One to change the light bulb and one to look bored."

—Neil Tennant, Pet Shop Boys

"I hope they don't think we're a rock and roll outfit."

—Mick Jagger, 1962

"I would like to eventually turn into Germaine Greer."

—Morrissey, 1986

"Our basic philosophy is that we like very heavy emotions—like fear and war—but sometimes we just try to create craziness."

—Daniel B, Front 242, 1989

"I'm just not that interested in rock music, even though sometimes it's exactly what I do."

—Neal Schon, Journey

"What I'm really lookin' for is this big hand to come out of the sky and say, 'Just sit around in your apartment—here's $200 or $300 a week to do it.'"

—Julia Cafritz, Pussy Galore, 1987

"I perceive of myself more as a Tarzan than as a singer anyway."

—David Lee Roth, 1984

JOHN LYDON: We ain't no band, we're a company. Simple—nothin' to do with rock 'n' roll. Doo dah.
TOM SNYDER: Doo dah?
LYDON: Yeah.

—"Tomorrow," 1980

"All three rhythms inside of me—the critic, the artist, the people—have one goal: total abandon, total communication, and to be truly, totally ready to go into the spinning fluid void where the light flakes and lands·on the banks of pleasure."

—Patti Smith, 1977

"I think Yes is kind of interesting...it's a kind of school."

—Patrick Moraz, Yes, 1976

"At the moment I have no time for acting, but when it's all over I think I'd like to go to drama school. I rather go for the contemporaries, like the John Cassavetes film *Shadows*; there was no script, the whole thing was ad-libbed."

—Mick Jagger, 1966

"I start two new pictures early next year. And I think maybe one day I'd like to do a singing-boxer film."

—Elvis Presley, 1957

"There's good music and there's bad music. I intend to spend a lot of time in the former category."

—Felix Pappalardi, Mountain, 1970

"I don't understand it. All we're trying to do is destroy everything."

—Johnny Rotten, 1977

PRETZEL LOGIC
(GOBBLEDYGOOK)

"I am a dialectician, so I can only talk in the abstract. What's your name? Your name must be Bob."

—Nico, 1979

"'Inductive Reasoning' is a term from systems theory. It's the measure of a system's capacity to withstand perturbations within the system. In other words, a system which has a high measure of inductive resonance will be able to withstand a high degree of oscillation among its components and still maintain the essential integrity of the system—contradiction, in other words."

—Robert Fripp, 1981

ROLLING STONE: What is the strangest thing that ever happened to you?
BOB DYLAN: You're gonna get it, man.
ROLLING STONE: What is the weirdest thing that ever happened to you?
DYLAN: I'll talk to you about it later. I wouldn't do that to you.

—1968

"I had lived in Texas and I had seen his name on some country jukeboxes and I wondered how in the world a hillbilly could be the next big thing, especially with a name like Elvis Presley. Anyway, Elvis came in wearing some odd-looking clothes. I said, 'Hello, Elvis, I'm Pat Boone.' He just said, 'Mrrrbleee mrrrbleee.'"

—Pat Boone, 1991

"There's nothing worse than hearing Phil Collins, day after day, all the time. It makes me sick, and I love the guy. It makes him sick, and he loves him. 'Cause he's him! You hear what I'm saying?"

—Mark Holmes, Platinum Blonde, 1988

"I'm not consciously *anything*. I'm not even conscious of being unconscious."

—Lee Michaels, 1974

"The longer I stay in this, the more I don't know. I used to think that I knew, but I don't know. I know enough to know that I don't know. I know that might sound confusing to you."

—Blackie Lawless, W.A.S.P., 1987

WOMEN AND CHILDREN FIRST
(GROUPIES)

"We really don't attract groupies. There was one night in Wolverhampton when we got to the gig and there were lines of teenage girls outside. We thought our luck had changed until the doorman explained that the Backstreet Boys were playing in a bigger hall upstairs."

—Jeff Tweedy, Wilco, 1999

"As Britain's unlikely new sex God, I sleep with lots of women. Where do you think I get my songs from?"

—Jarvis Cocker, Pulp, 1996

"Let's face it, if I was a dentist it wouldn't be quite the same. If there are uglier guys around I don't know where they are, and yet I am the King of Pussy. It's the biggest kick."

—Gene Simmons, Kiss

"Mostly we end up finding that we don't get the pussy."

—MCA, Beastie Boys, 1986

"If a woman is with me because I'm L.L. Cool J, she's *right*. I *am* L.L. Cool J."

—L.L. Cool J, 1992

"We were out doing a couple of nights opening for Johnny Thunders. These girls show up and want to come backstage and just say 'Hi' to Johnny. He was all upset that they weren't back there for more than that. I was sitting there going, 'Oh, dear God, please don't ever let us mutate into anything remotely like this.'"

—Rodney Anonymous, Dead Milkmen, 1990

"I've always fancied the idea of some chick coming in, trashing the place to my music, and then trying to screw you to death. There's certainly nothing wrong with that."

—Billy Idol, 1990

"We're all very afraid of catching venereal disease, but there were so many girls who were willing to be with us that we had to kind of tap the energy."
—Barry Henssler, Necros, 1988

"You wake up one day and go: 'Ugh!' It's like: 'OK, OK, so now I've shagged every bird in North America, that's kind of boring, let's get into a relationship.'"
—Lars Ulrich, Metallica, 1996

"Any guy in a band will take any girl who offers herself. Doesn't matter if she's a farmyard animal."
—Chrissie Hynde, the Pretenders, 1999

"I'm still searching for an angel with a broken wing. It's not very easy to find them these days. Especially when you're staying at the Plaza Hotel."
—Jimmy Page, 1975

"I can't say once in a while I haven't taken a fuckin' blow job. There, that's perfect for your article."
—Fred Durst, Limp Bizkit, 2000

"Of course there were Monkees groupies, but I don't know, the events of the day seem so harmless in retrospect. I mean, we really were innocent guys. I'm sure there wasn't half a homosexual among the whole crew, and if there was it was evenly distributed."
—Peter Tork, the Monkees, 1986

"We've been very fortunate in a sense that girls like our band, so we have a lot of girls come to see our band and there are a lot of very attractive girls and there's monsters and there's freaks and everything in between and that can be really fun. And so we've had fun."
—Ricki Rockett, Poison, 2000

"We came to the States and it was unbelievable. I was very interested in meeting girls—the more the morrior. I took care of myself. I avoided the drugs. I would go to parties with other rock 'n' roll musicians, and they would all sit in one room smoking dope with the blinds closed, being very serious and talking about the war in Vietnam, and in the meantime I was in another room with all their girlfriends."

—Peter Noone, Herman's Hermits, 1988

OUR LITTLE GROUP HAS ALWAYS BEEN AND ALWAYS WILL
(GROUPS)

"Being in a gang and being in a band are completely different things. Gangs usually fight over really, really important things like, 'You're hanging out on my block,' whereas bands usually fight over much more important issues like, 'You stole the banana from my dressing room.'"

—John "Speedo" Reis, Rocket From the Crypt, 1996

"With the group, everyone is one and no one is the leader. It is not like Eric Burdon *and* the Animals, it's just *the* Iron Butterfly and that's the way we dig it."

—Doug Ingle, Iron Butterfly, 1969

"My daddy, Elvis Presley, came to me and said, 'Son, I want you to sing Led Zeppelin's music the way it was supposed to be done—reggae style.'"

—Tortelvis, Dread Zeppelin, 1990

"We were both living in old cars outside of Palo Alto. Jerry happened to have a huge tin of pineapple chunks, and I had a glove compartment full of spoons. We became a sort of symbiotic unit."

—Robert Hunter, Grateful Dead lyricist, 1973

"I don't see how groups do it when they're asked, 'How did you get together?' and somebody goes, 'Well, I was working in a paint store and Jimmy was my roommate and we both dug guitars'—that's about the most literal kind of way that somebody gets together. If you're existing on that level, that's fine. But we don't. I was *born* Devo. I went to church every week for fifteen years with Mr. Potato Head."

—Mark Mothersbaugh, Devo, 1979

"Paul McCartney at one time was very concerned about our career, and he wrote us a letter saying that we had to drop the Byrds glasses and the twelve-string. No alternatives suggested.

Merely just get rid of them. A very cryptic note actually."

—Roger McGuinn, the Byrds, 1970

"Sid's the philosopher of the band."

—Johnny Rotten, 1977

I'M NOT SICK, BUT I'M NOT WELL
(HEALTH)

"Most of us are veggie, which means when you're abroad you just point at the thing with cheese in and hope."

—Brett Anderson, Suede, 1997

"On a physical level, I find that something called ginger root helps. I make a tea from that and then add honey to it and it's really excellent for the vocal cords. You know, it's amazing, ginger has so many healthy properties that they haven't even begun to discover yet."

—Paul Rodgers, Bad Company, 2000

"Yoga interests me a lot. Everything is yoga. Music is a kind of yoga."

—Jah Wobble, 1994

"The yoga centre was shut today, so I took full advantage and went to the pub."

—Sting, 1996

"I think fresh air might kill me."

—Sid Vicious, 1978

"I'm not going to the doctor, I'd rather die."

—Johnny Rotten, 1977

"I was sick, and Prince brought some cough syrup up to my hotel room. He was sweet—he walked around the room folding things, fluffing pillows, tidying up in general. Then he gave me a spoon of it himself. But when I asked for another spoonful, he changed—he said, 'I didn't come all the way up here to get you hooked on another substance!' Then he left."

—Stevie Nicks, 1994

"I have problems just like everyone else. I told myself when I finished my first solo album, *It Takes a Thief*, 'I'mma quit smoking.' Then it was, 'When I go gold, I'll quit smoking.' Then it was, 'If I go platinum, I'll quit smoking.' Now it's just, 'Damn, I wish I could quit smoking.'"

—Coolio, 1995

THE BALLAD OF TOMMY LEE AND JUDAS PRIEST
(HEAVY METAL)

"We really are idiots, genuine idiots! We love metal, we love stupid heavy metal, we're aware that it's stupid heavy metal, but we love it all the same and we want to be in a stupid heavy metal band. We're kind of an intelligent stupid metal band, really."

—Mark Manning, Zodiac Mindwarp, 1988

"We maintain a lead guitar and a bass guitar, because you just need that *ker-RANG*."

—Ali Score, A Flock of Seagulls, 1983

"If you're into heavy metal, you must have a heavy metal plate in what's left of your burned-out brain."

—Jim McDonnell, Stray Cats, 1983

"I am really grossly offended by Led Zeppelin, not only because they're total charlatans and thieves, but because it actually embarrasses me."

—Elvis Costello, 1986

"None of us have quit our day jobs; we're still grounded in reality, because you know that death metal doesn't pay the bills and you gotta work for a living like everyone else."

—Karl Sanders, Nile, 2000

"That's why we've lasted so long—we're not fashionable. Whitesnake's never been about production companies and Swiss mime artists. We're certainly not heavy metal—the only thing metal about Whitesnake is the guitar strings."

—David Coverdale, Whitesnake, 1982

"Sweden also has *great* heavy metal bands, like Meshuggah, Hellacopters, and Battery. Meshuggah are so extremely heavy that you can't even listen to them."

—Nina Persson, the Cardigans, 1998

EPISTLE TO HIPPIE

"I always believed for many years that when people love to work for you, baby, you can get the best out of them. And we get in there, and when those string men come in there, sometimes thirty, sometimes twenty, everybody's 'How ya doin' Barry baby?' I feed everybody, I just dig people."

—Barry White, 1974

"I've seen Crosby, Stills and Nash burnin' ass. They're groovy. Yeah. Western sky music. All delicate and ding-ding-ding-ding."

—Jimi Hendrix, 1970

"I think I know what you like, baby. I say I think, I think I say, I know there ain't nobody out there come to be mellow tonight, now did you? I say there ain't *nobody* out there that even wants to be a little mellow, now is there?"

—Ted Nugent, *Double-Live Gonzo*, 1978

ALVY: Did you go to a rock concert?
ANNIE: Yeah.
ALVY: Oh yeah, really? Really? How—how'd you like it? Was it—was it, I mean, did it...was it heavy? Did it achieve total heaviosity?

—*Annie Hall*, 1977

"Rock 'n' roll seemed like a step backwards. Occasionally it peaks, and some wonderful things have come out of it, but for the most part the music is mediocre bullshit, you dig?"

—Al Jarreau, 1988

"Um, you know, I can sit up here all night and say thank-you-thank-you-thank-you, you know, but at this stage I just wanna graaaab ya, man, and just ooooooohhh. One of them things, man, one of them scenes. But dig, I just can't *do* that."

—Jimi Hendrix, *Jimi Plays Monterey*, 1967

"The people who are digging Hendrix are digging him for different reasons than I dig him. Most people dig him because of his sensational showmanship...If that gives them just a little more pleasure than they would have got out of the music by itself, I can dig it. I'm a musician, and I can see what Jimi Hendrix is doing musically and I dig that, too."

—Elvin Bishop, 1970

"Sly's my idea of a beautiful group. They get me off. Like very few people get me off as a group, as a total thing. No individual cat, but as a total thing. They really get me off."

—Marty Balin, Jefferson Airplane, 1970

I'M HENRY VIII, I AM
(HISTORY LESSON)

"Wow! Paul McCartney! I read about you in history class."

—Lisa Simpson, 1995

"I mean, there's no doubt that the Beatles took pop music into another realm. It had to happen, someone had to do it, and they did it. It couldn't have been us because we started too early. But we were pioneers, and they came after the pioneers, built upon the foundation, and took it soaring away."

—Cliff Richard, 1988

"Wasn't nothin' before me but cows and hogs and chickens!"
—Little Richard, 1987

"The Feelgoods really started the New Wave, a lot more than most people seem to think. They were definitely the first New Wave band. Everybody says it was the Pistols who started it, but I couldn't really see the Pistols happening without the Feelgoods happening first."

—Joe Jackson, 1979

"It's like buying a piece of Sigue Sigue Sputnik, a piece of the event, a piece of history."

—Martin Degville, 1986

"Rock and roll had become stagnant in 1985. 'Achy Breaky Heart' was seven years away; something had to fill the void. That something was barbershop."

—Homer Simpson, 1993

"The Beatles put a class element into rock 'n' roll because they were British. The President's daughters—Johnson's daughters—came to see them. All of a sudden you were in an art form. Crazy, isn't it?"

—Phil Everly, 1981

"Las Vegas is a town that never should have happened. It was started by a guy called Moe Greene, who wanted a stopping-off place for servicemen on their way to California, and it took off like a virus."

—Tom Waits, 1987

"Why do you need new bands? Everyone knows rock attained perfection in 1974. It's a scientific fact."

—Homer Simpson, 1996

SOME BOYS NAMED SUE
(HOMOSEXUALITY)

"If I didn't know me, I'd probably think I was gay too."

—Sisqo, 2000

"Playing with Joe Perry really gets me off. I'm not gay, but I love him."

—Steven Tyler, Aerosmith, 1994

"I'm pretty much over my affection for me. The only time I get halfway wistful for those old days is in Japan. All those little boys are so cute, I just want to take them *all* up to my room."

—David Bowie, 1976

"I can't wait to see Japan—all those Geisha girls and boys!"

—Freddie Mercury, 1981

"Actually, I've found that a lot of lesbians really like Julie Andrews. She's one of the 'people,' you know. One of our icons."

—k.d. lang, 1995

"I really dig David Bowie. I like his songs and we have a very good head thing...but we don't make love. To make love wouldn't be repulsive to me, it would just be a bit of a bore...and it would hurt."

—Marc Bolan, T. Rex, 1973

"I don't go into the bathroom in the morning and say, 'Hey, I'm a woman, aren't I beautiful?' I'm a man. And very much a man. I have a hairy chest, you know."

—Boy George, 1984

"What I'm actually saying is, I am gay, and I have written songs from that point of view. So, I mean, I'm being surprisingly honest with you here, but those are the facts of the matter. Well, what's your next question?"

—Neil Tennant, Pet Shop Boys, 1994

"We're six very positive male symbols. We're definitely gonna have a gay following."

—Glenn Hughes, the Village People, 1979

"I would say that the Navy has an interest in communicating opportunities in the service, and the Village People seem to fit in very well with young people."

—Lieutenant Commander Fred Gorell, Navy spokesman, 1979

"In England they have only one Queen, those poor guys. I mean, in New York we've got millions of queens."

—Sylvain Sylvain, New York Dolls, 1978

"I suppose to the local plumber I'm a screaming queen, but then it's all relative, isn't it? I'm not 'homosexual'—but then I'm not 'heterosexual,' either. I mean, having sex with boys or girls is like eating a bag of crisps to me."

—Boy George, 1983

"Some of these bands you see on TV, you think it's a fucking chick and it turns out to be a guy—shit, it flips me out. I think Boy George wears those clothes 'cause he's too fat. My old lady goes out and buys all those albums."

—Eddie Money, 1984

"Arnold Layne just happens to dig dressing up in women's clothing. A lot of people do—so let's face up to reality."
—Syd Barrett, Pink Floyd, 1967

"I had a bit of a crush on Billy Bragg...I mean, you can't help it, can you? He's pretty irresistible."
—Jimmy Somerville, Bronski Beat

"It's amazing how many people I see in London who look like me. Even girls!"
—Grace Jones, 1985

"I was always considered middle-class faggy until I moved to Liverpool. Then I met Pete Burns and Holly Johnson, and they thought I was a real brute."
—Julian Cope, the Teardrop Explodes, 1987

"I don't mind kissing men at all, though it's not as easy as kissing women...But I don't wank over men. If you think about men when you're on your own and you want to have a wank, then you've got an interest in men which is homosexual."
—Damon Albarn, Blur, 1995

"Every straight guy should have a man's tongue in his mouth at least once."
—Madonna, 1991

"I'm fey and I'm effeminate and I really can't do much about it."
—Brett Anderson, Suede, 1996

"We asked Prince if he would be our December cover and he said we'd have to talk to his manager and we said that we'd asked the manager and the manager said to ask him, and so they said they'd work it out. We were just shaking, it was so exciting. And Billy Idol was there and you know, seeing these two glamour boys, it's like boys are the new Hollywood glamour girls, like Harlow and Marilyn. So weird."
—*The Andy Warhol Diaries*, 1986

"Gays are great to poke fun at. They're a great source of humor; they should be harangued a little more."

—Lee Ving, Fear, 1982

PLAYBOY: Do you get off on the bisexuality scene?
ELTON JOHN: Ah, I sort of got pneumonia sitting out in this theater last night. So fucking cold....And, um, I played tennis on the court the other night. It was so foggy I couldn't see the other players.

—1976

GERMFREE ADOLESCENTS
(HYGIENE)

"Lemmy's quite clean. He has a bath every night on tour."

—Kim McAuliffe, Girlschool

"Lemmy gave me a drink out of his bottle once, and for weeks later I was worried that I'd caught some godawful disease."

—Michael Gerald/Bill Hobson/Dan Hobson, Killdozer, 1988

"Everybody vomits now and again."

—Johnny Rotten, 1978

"I never sing in the shower 'cos I never shower. But we do have a bath that vibrates at G-flat. So I do a lot of vocal mantras in the style of Sly Stone on *There's a Riot Goin' On*."

—Julian Cope, 1997

"I don't change me socks as often as I ought to. That's not too bad, is it? It's not like I'm a heroin addict."

—Jarvis Cocker, Pulp, 1996

TOMBSTONE BLUES
(IMMORTALITY)

"I'm worried about when I kick off. Will anybody notice it? That's something to think about, you know—will anybody notice when Bo Diddley ceases to exist?"

—Bo Diddley, 1988

"I don't believe in death. Death is just a thing, whatever it is."

—Liam Gallagher, Oasis, 1995

"I love cemeteries. I'm always walking around saying, 'Hi, how are you doing?' to the graves, because I feel there's so much energy there."

—Sophie B. Hawkins, 1995

"I'm a tryer. I'm not somebody who's into saying, 'I can't do it.' I guess that's what they'll write on my tombstone: 'HE TRIED.'"

—Ice-T, 1995

"People, whether they know it or not, like their blues singers miserable. They like their blues singers to die afterwards."

—Janis Joplin

"What's that? Elvis Presley died?...Makes you feel sad, doesn't it? Like your grandfather died...Yeah, it's just too bad it couldn't have been Mick Jagger."

—Malcolm McLaren, Sex Pistols manager, 1977

TOMMY MOTTOLA GETS HIS TONSILS OUT
(THE INDUSTRY)

"I buy a lot of records. I'm personally keeping the record industry afloat!"

—Elvis Costello, 1983

"You can have but so much freedom. I could say I want to do a record that says 'Fuck-fuck-fuck-fuck-fuck-fuck-fuck-fuck-fuck-fuck-fuck-fuck-fuck' for five minutes, and they'll say, 'Well, can you say one less "fuck?"' You know what I'm saying?"

—Schoolly-D, 1988

"When I first got to the States, the record company asked me to brush me hair down and be like David Cassidy, or that guy from 'General Hospital.' They showed me this picture and asked 'Will you be him?' This is me own management talking. And I said 'NO WAY!'"

—Billy Idol, 1990

"We're not adopting a theory against the music biz. We're not like Chumbawumba or whatever."

—Richard Greentree, Beta Band, 1999

"RCA is in a panic. They don't know how to copyright this. How do you take musical notation on it? I said, 'Look, don't worry. Nobody's gonna cover it.' I can't see the Carpenters doing their version of it."

—Lou Reed on *Metal Machine Music*, 1975

"We wanted to call it *The Joshua Bush*, but for some reason the record company didn't want us to."

—Rodney Anonymous, Dead Milkmen, 1987

"The industry is just rife with jealousy and hatred. Everybody in it is a failed bassist."

—Morrissey, 1985

YOU'RE THE INSPIRATION
(INSPIRATIONS)

"I remember the first time I saw Chicago...This is right after their first album. I got a big knot in my stomach. I couldn't believe this band. I was so into Blood, Sweat and Tears for a long time. Then all of a sudden a group like Chicago comes along...God, I always wanted to play with a band like that."

—Bobby Kimball, Toto, 1983

"Poco had Hollywood set on fire when they were first together. I've told you before about how I used to hang around them and watch them rehearse with my mouth hanging open."

—Glenn Frey, Eagles, 1973

"M.C. Hammer was the James Brown of our generation! He was the hardest-working man in show business. Then the whole world got tired of him, you know."

—Darryl McDaniels, Run-D.M.C., 1998

"In 1976 I was 10 years old, and the stuff you like as a kid, that makes an impression on you, is not the same music you're gonna like when you're older. 'You Make Me Feel Like Dancing' by Leo Sayer reminds me of pissing my pants in Woolworths trying to find a toilet. I bought the record 'cos I needed a pee!"

—Ben Folds, 1997

"You ever hear pygmy music? Check that out. You ever hear the music of the Montagnard of Vietnam?"

—Jonathan Richman, 1985

"I remember going to see T. Rex in Cleveland. Marc Bolan weighed 300 pounds and came out in this batwing costume and beat his guitar with a whip. 'Holy shit,' I thought, 'this guy is my idol!'"

—Lux Interior, the Cramps, 1980

"When I saw Blue Oyster Cult, I was on the ground floor. Ted Nugent came on first, Kansas after that, and when BOC came out it just blew—it was, like, rock!"

—D. Boon, the Minutemen, 1985

"When I'm doing a Michael Jackson song, I think I *am* him. I become him."

—R. Kelly, 2001

INTERVIEWER: Who do you think is the best folk singer in the world?
BOB DYLAN: Oh, Peter Lorre.

—1966

"All around, 13 was a really strange year...My brother used to like Captain Beefheart, Nick Drake. I used to know all the words to *Safe as Milk*. He used to sing me to sleep with it."

—Robert Smith, the Cure, 1987

"Björk is seen as the Icelandic elf child-woman. But Björk wants to be seen as more erotic. And I'm like, 'Why?' Elf child-woman is a *good* job."

—Courtney Love, 1994

"Michael Jackson, he used to watch me from the wings and got his moon walk from my camel walk. I ain't jealous, I'm zealous. I ain't teased, I'm *pleased*."

—James Brown, 1986

63

"In fact, I idolized them. John Lennon drank Bacardi and Coke and smoked Lark cigarettes. For five years after I found that out, I only drank Bacardi and Coke and smoked Lark cigarettes."
—Peter Noone, Herman's Hermits, 1988

NERVE!: What about someone like Alan Vega? He's really mad you took all his stuff.
MARTIN DEGVILLE: Took all his stuff?
NERVE!: Yeah, you did.
DEGVILLE: No we didn't.
NERVE!: Yes you did.
DEGVILLE: No we didn't.
NERVE!: Yes you did.
DEGVILLE: No way.
—1986

"When I was nine, about the coolest thing I was listening to was Dr. Hook and the Medicine Show because they were on 'The Midnight Special.'"
—Michael Gerald/Bill Hobson/Dan Hobson, Killdozer, 1988

HOMER SIMPSON: You know, my kids think you're the greatest. And thanks to your gloomy music, they've finally stopped dreaming of a future I can't possibly provide.
BILLY CORGAN: Well, we try to make a difference.
—"The Simpsons," 1996

"I'm a big Styx fan! If Dennis DeYoung had sung for Led Zeppelin, it would have been a whole different story. They would have sold one record—to me!"
—Brian Vander Ark, Verve Pipe, 1999

EDUMACATION AIN'T FOR ME!
(INTELLIGENCE)

"We never wrote songs that were above people's heads."
—Joey Ramone, 1986

"The biggest misconception people have about me is that I'm stupid."
—Billy Idol

"I still like black music, disco music…'Shame, Shame, Shame' or 'Rock Your Baby'—I'd give my eye-tooth to have written that. But I never could. I am too literal to write 'Rock Your Baby.' I wish I could. I'm too intellectual, even though I'm not really an intellectual."

—John Lennon, 1975

"We've barely tapped the powers of the mind."

—Elvis Presley

"I wonder if all the people who buy the records really understand the meaning that I've given it. You know, you analyze poetry in school and the nice liberal teachers say, 'Well, anything you can get out of it is nice.' But I always like it best when people get what I try to do."

—Randy Newman, 1973

"Smart people are highly overrated."

—Cher, 1995

**"I think brains have gotten in the way of too many things."
—Keith Richards, 1977**

"I've got a brain."
—Christina Aguilera, 2000

"I really like clowns. I think they're brilliant people."
—Andy Bell, Erasure, 1995

REPORTER: What do you expect to find here in Australia?
JOHN LENNON: Australians, I should think.

—1964

YOU TALKIN' TO ME?
(INTERVIEWS)

"Let's wail, babe!"

—Huey Lewis, 1986

"Will you do me a favor? Could you please try and make my quotes as concise as you can? Sometimes I have a tendency to, uh, ramble."

—Eddie Vedder, Pearl Jam, 1994

"Come to the teepee. I'll tell you everything you want to know."

—Felipe, the Village People, 1996

"All we ever get asked are loads of tedious questions about our music, influences, and record collections. You know, we've been asked our opinion on Spencer Davis. How exciting can you make that?"

—Steve Cradock, Ocean Colour Scene, 1996

"Come on, ask us some more poxy, uninteresting questions."

—John Lydon, 1984

"I like *Graffiti*, it's very nice. It's a hip magazine, and I too was puzzled as to why you were interested in putting me on the cover."

—Barry Manilow, 1988

"That didn't hurt a bit. The people's right to know!"

—Huey Lewis, 1986

MY DEFINITION OF A BOOMBASTIC JAZZ STYLE
(JAZZ)

"I don't think jazz has *ever* appealed to the younger generation...I mean, what would some parent say to his kid if the kid came home with a glass eye, a Charlie Mingus record, and a pocketful of feathers? He'd say, 'Who are you following?' And the poor kid would have to stand there with water in his shoes, a bow tie on his ear, and soot pouring out of his belly button and say, 'Jazz, Father, I've been following jazz.'"

—Bob Dylan, 1966

"I'm trying to use jazz now in way that will work commercially. Not like Herbie Hancock or John McLaughlin just catering for one section of the public. Our rock sounds will be Zeppelinish and the jazz side will verge on the Stan Kenton. We don't want people to get confused."

—Roy Wood, 1976

"I always considered the Stooges a jazz band more than a rock band."

—Iggy Pop, 1979

"The only people I've seen lately are Grace Jones and some disgusting hippie, this terrible pox, a boil on the backside of the universe, this jazz twat with long curly hair named Pat Metheny. You ought to have seen the looks when I walked into Town Hall to see him. All he did was cover all the popular themes and melodies you hear in advertisements, bullshitted up with loads of twaddly bits on guitar...One of his songs was based entirely on that commercial jingle, 'Red Lobster for the seafood lover in you.'"

—John Lydon, 1981

"This guy George Benson, years ago, he was a bass player, invented the Benson amplifier, absolutely no distortion, totally clean, totally pure sound. It's interesting what Hancock's doing with the Arp."

—Lou Reed, 1975

FIRST MAN: I think Stubby's gone overboard with those altered chords, don't you?

FIRST WOMAN: I agree. I think Brubeck and Desmond have gone just as far with dissonance as I care to go.

SECOND MAN: Oh, nonsense! Have you heard Lennie Tristano's latest recording? He reached outer-space!

SECOND WOMAN: Someday they'll make the cycle and get back to pure old Dixieland. I say atonality is just a passing phase in jazz music. What do you think, Mr. Everett?

VINCE EVERETT: Lady, I don't know what the hell you're talking about.

—Elvis Presley as Vince Everett, *Jailhouse Rock*, 1957

JESUS AND MARY CHAIN ARE JUST ALRIGHT WITH ME

"Jesus Christ has been followed and preached about for 2,000 years, and people seriously think that this little group making a fairly obscure little record called 'Jesus Suck' is going to do anybody any harm whatsoever?"

—Jim Reid, Jesus and Mary Chain, 1986

"The Jesus and Mary Chain are like fourth-form Velvets without Lou. You know, there's just nothing there. You can't grab hold of it. I know what they're trying to do, but they're just so bad, y'know."

—David Bowie, 1987

"I like what the Jesus and Mary Chain is trying to do, but their act is bullshit to me. The singer gets down on the floor, but he doesn't belong down on the floor; he doesn't go down gracefully, he doesn't get up gracefully. He goes down *gradually*, like he's afraid he's gonna hurt himself."

—Alan Vega, Suicide, 1988

Q: Jungle?
MORRISSEY: Jungle! I don't know what that is.
Q: It's someone shouting incomprehensibly over mechanical rhythms.
MORRISSEY: But I thought that was the Jesus and Mary Chain.

—1995

WE KNOCKED 'EM DEAD IN DALLAS
(JEWISHNESS)

"About halfway through the show I started *kibitzing* with somebody in the audience. Some girl started yelling requests. It was a small theater, and I had this whole conversation with her. She was just going on, and finally I said, 'These Jewish girls are just impossible to control.' And she yells out from the back, 'I'm not Jewish.' The audience fell down, and that broke the ice. I was actually saved by a *shiska* for the first time in my life."

—Neil Diamond, 1988

"I lived in Israel till I was nine, so I can *parlez-vous* the Hebrew."

—Gene Simmons, Kiss, 1998

"The Beatles...I'd just like to study their studies 'cos I know they've studied music backwards. That's how they get their music forwards. Music backwards is like Hebrew music forwards."

—Richie Havens, 1968

"I love all the races of people, from Arabs to Jewish people...My accountants and lawyers are Jewish."

—Michael Jackson, 1995

"We're playing a festival in Israel, an open-air festival. They love us there because of the Star of David—they *re-e-eally* love us there, it's *so* outrageous. We're doing an open-air festival for 8,000 people, it'll be brilliant. Amazing...there's not that many people in Israel, though, is there?"

—Boy George, 1983

WE AIN'T NO JOKE
(KEEPING IT REAL)

"We're in the age of keeping it real, but we're trying to keep it surreal. Real has got really boring."

—Andre 'Dre' Benjamin, Outkast, 2001

"We're putting a torch to all this wallpaper music that's around now."

—Bono, 1983

"I don't like to deal with reality, but I am an excellent driver."

—Prince Be, P.M. Dawn, 1993

"There's a difference between realness and an act, and Insane Clown Posse are an act, and they know they're an act, and they even say they're an act—they even say they're cornballs, they admit it."

—Eminem, 2000

"I'm not out to impress upon you how 'real' I am or how 'street' I am. I drink milk, I play Nintendo, you saw me reading the Sega magazine on the tour bus, and I don't have a problem with people seeing that side of me. Having said all that, though, I wouldn't advise you to fuck around with me."

—Ice-T, 1995

"I'm no transvestite. I don't set myself on fire. All I want to do is sing."

—Maria Muldaur, 1974

"We're not trying to be a pretty boy band or a fashion show. This is real."

—Robert Gordon, 1981

"We don't need a choir. We just turn this key, and there's the choir."

—Florian Schneider, Kraftwerk, 1975

"We're not going through the motions—or the emotions—that may be in fashion. And we're not a synthesizer band. You tell people that. Tell them we're NOT a synthesizer band."

—Bono, 1983

"If we mean 'Fuck your ass,' we say 'Fuck your ass.' We don't sing, 'Oh, oh, oh, let's sing like a faggot' and throw in maybe one dirty word on the whole album."

—Sickie Wifebeater, the Mentors, 1986

"I think I *am* quite a superficial person."

—Neil Tennant, Pet Shop Boys, 1989

B: What did those record company people want?
A: They want me to cut a record. They'll make my voice sound like it's singing.
—*The Philosophy of Andy Warhol*, 1976

"These stations that call themselves rock 'n' roll are playing a lot of this jerk music, like the music coming out of England now. Fuckin' cocksucking music. The average British musician should learn how to play his instrument before he goes up on stage."
—Ozzy Osbourne, 1984

"Anybody who tells you they didn't fix anything on a live album is strictly inaccurate."
—Joe Perry, Aerosmith, 1978

70

"There was a blues boom in Britain in the late '60s, but I found it very hard to go out and sing about how 'I left a steel mill in Chicago,' so I started singing about how 'I left my fish-and-chip shop in Brighton.'"

—Leo Sayer, 1988

"What I did with my Ziggy Stardust was package a totally credible, plastic rock 'n' roll singer—much better than what the Monkees could ever fabricate. I mean, my plastic rock 'n' roller was much more plastic than anybody's."

—David Bowie, 1976

"People didn't consider that I was actually real, that I could sit and talk and think."

—David Cassidy, 1985

"There's a thin line between what's hip and what's unhip. I like to walk that line."

—Stephen Bishop, 1978

"I'm not hip and I'm glad, because I hate hip. Hip doesn't last. I was never hip."

—Meat Loaf, 1983

"Hip means being now. I don't want to be now. I want to be forever."

—Lionel Richie, 1996

BASED ON A NOVEL BY A MAN NAMED LEAR
(LITERACY)

"*Extended Sexual Orgasm* is the book the Beastie Boys live by. MCA read it the most times; he read it once."

—King Ad-Rock, Beastie Boys, 1987

"Poets usually have very unhappy endings. Look at Keats' life. Look at Jim Morrison, if you want to call him a poet. Look at him. Although some people say that he really is in the Andes."

—Bob Dylan, 1991

"Mostly I read menus and traffic signs and that's about it."

—David Yow, Jesus Lizard, 1996

"And, anyway, Shakespeare was much more violent than Alice Cooper ever was. In fact, I think if Shakespeare was around today, he'd be one of my biggest fans. I think Walt Disney would, too, but I don't think I would let Pat Boone's daughter into one of my shows."

—Alice Cooper, 1975

"I did Shakespeare. Now I come from nowhere but the streets and I'd never read Shakespeare until I acted it, and people had told me it was so difficult. But to me it was the easiest thing in the world to understand, because he was coming from the same level. It's just that it's written old-fashioned."

—Meat Loaf, 1978

"I always think of 'Werewolves of London' as a dumb song for smart people, though there are times when I realize that what people like about me may not be as refined and intellectual as I pretended it was. It has more to do with their response to that gonzo party guy, y'know, the 'evil Jimmy Buffet.' I thought I was the rock 'n' roll Nabokov, not the 'evil Buffet'!"

—Warren Zevon, 1995

"I'm afraid I always wanted to be a librarian. To me that seemed like the perfect life: solitude; absolute silence; tall, dark libraries. But then they started to become very modern, you know, these little pre-fabs, and they had no romance whatsoever."

—Morrissey, 1985

"I like opera! A lot! I read books. Lots of 'em! All the time!"

—Iggy Pop, 1988

"I like the bible as a book. Just like I like *The Cat in the Hat*."

—Marilyn Manson

"It can be a bit of a pointless task learning a lot, because there's always someone who's going to know that bit more. So, if ever you've got an opinion, there's probably someone around who's got a different opinion based upon a greater bit of knowledge. So this pursuit of knowledge can be a complete and utter waste of time."

—Chris Lowe, Pet Shop Boys, 1989

"I'm exactly the man who Friedrich Nietzsche could only write about."

—Iggy Pop, 1979

"If ever I see Tennessee Williams' play *Orpheus Descending*, I think Elvis would have been the best person to play that part."

—Quentin Tarantino, 1995

ROLLING STONE: What poets do you dig?
BOB DYLAN: Rimbaud, I guess; W.C. Fields; the family, you know, the trapeze family in the circus."

—1968

WE GET PAID TO DO THE WILD THING
(THE LIVE EXPERIENCE)

"When I'm onstage, it's me up there."

—Lene Lovich, 1980

"I once saw Pink Floyd build a table on stage, miking the hammers and saws, and then hammering or sawing in rhythm. Then they sat around the table and drank tea. That was the first industrial performance I ever saw."

—Genesis P-Orridge, Psychic TV, 1988

"I have to get a band together to come on tour. I'm trying to find people who'll move around a lot, because when I'm on stage, I don't at all. It's partly to do with my shyness and partly, I suppose, just because I'm an idiot."

—Sinead O'Connor, 1988

"There were lots of bands at Woodstock, that's for sure, but only about fifty people in the audience, and most of them were crew, girlfriends, people working for the promoter, relatives of Mike Lang...Only about three people paid. Loretta Johnson paid. I don't remember the other two."

—Country Joe McDonald, 1994

"There's no magic anymore. When I saw the *Foxtrot* tour with Genesis, Peter Gabriel walked out with bat wings on his head and a little bit of fluorescent paint around his eyes. It was theatre, creating new spaces. Zodiac Mindwarp walks on with Nazi fuckin' swastikas on his jacket, and skullcrosses and switchblades up his nose. That's not the same thing as batwings and fluorescent paint around your eyes, I'm sorry."

—Ivan Doroschuk, Men Without Hats, 1988

"I went to see Grand Funk Railroad under the influence of some kind of narcotic, and walked out in the first song. Mark Farner walked on with his shirt off, with these two big metal bands on his arms. He flexed his arms, popped the bands off, and as soon as the bands popped off, the group went BOOM! into 'We're an American Band.' That was just a little bit much."

—Peter Buck, R.E.M., 1985

"Most of the time you really don't know where you are. It's very possible that you may come out on stage and say, 'It's great to be here in St. Louis' and you could very well be in Denver or Seattle. That's happened."

—Tom Waits, 1985

"We played with Skinny Puppy once. Lots of blood like Kiss, with TV sets. Yeah, they're like Kiss for hair farmers."

—Michael Gerald/Bill Hobson/Dan Hobson, Killdozer, 1988

"When the rocket was going to the moon, I was so emotionally excited…When I saw this on television, I thought it was one of the best performances I had ever seen."

—Ralf Hutter, Kraftwerk, 1975

INTERNATIONAL TIMES: How do you feel when students riot when you're on stage? Do you pick up any energy?
MICK JAGGER: Yes! Wow! Tingle with it!

—1968

"We confused a lot of people. The audience would literally scream at us, boo, throw bottles. It got to the stage that we'd have to pretend to be a covers band in order to get shows. So we'd come on and I'd say, 'This is a song by Bad Company,' and we'd go straight into the usual Devo stuff."

—Gerald Casale, Devo, 2000

"I've learnt something at every show. There's no substitution for getting a bottle in the head at the wrong angle and having to keep singing."

—Adam Ant, 1981

"Thank you very much the person who threw this glass bottle at my head—you nearly killed me, but you missed again, so you have to keep trying again next week."

—Iggy Pop, *Metallic K.O.*, 1976

MOST OF THEM ARE BEAUTIFUL BUT SO OBSESSED WITH GLOOM
(LONELINESS)

"I get lonesome sometimes. I get lonesome right in the middle of a crowd."

—Elvis Presley

"My ultimate city dwelling would be a concrete bunker which you drive straight into and shut off the world outside."

—Chris Lowe, Pet Shop Boys, 1993

"Sometimes I get a little sad, because I look out into that audience and I know it's not going to be there for very long, that the moment is going to be gone."

—Billy Corgan, Smashing Pumpkins, 1994

"I'll miss you, Pumpkins, but I just can't share your bleak worldview. I've got too much to live for."

—Homer Simpson, 1996

"I feel very safe in cars. You can lock the doors and they can't get to you. I don't like people getting' to me...People will hurt me."

—Gary Numan, 1980

THEY WANT TO KNOW WHAT LOVE IS
(LOVE)

"If I fall in love tomorrow with a guy who runs McDonald's, I'm going to follow my heart."

—Britney Spears, 1999

75

"I might be married, I might not. It's hard to explain really."

—Bob Dylan, 1966

"If you're asking if there's going to be any Yoko Ono action in this band, the answer is no."

—Zac Hanson

"David Bowie called and told me that he was really in love with his wife. Don't know why he called to tell me that but he did."

—Macy Gray, 2000

"I'm tired of people usin' the word 'love' so much, though. You can mess up a good theme like that. I don't know, we can go on and on and on."

—Jimi Hendrix, 1970

"It's a proven fact: Most people who say 'I love you' don't mean it. Doctors have proved that."

—Bob Dylan, 1991

"I was in love when I was 16, but since then I can't say I have been. There's been girls that when they're *not* there in the room, I've been thinking about them like, 'Ummmmmmmmmmm.' But as soon as they're in the room with me, it gets kind of sour. I can love them providing they don't come near me."

—Joe Strummer, the Clash, 1977

EXILES IN GUYVILLE
(MASCULINITY)

"Blur are not lads. Pearl Jam are not lads. Stone Temple Pilots are not fucking lads. The Who were lads. The Sex Pistols were lads. Suede are not lads. Are you starting to get the drift now? Frankie Goes to Hollywood were not lads."

—Liam Gallagher, Oasis, 1995

"I got accused of being a male chauvinist pig, which I am."

—Mac Davis, 1973

"Everything we do, we try to be very masculine in our movements. That's why we have taken up karate to replace choreography and dancing."

—Alan Osmond, 1973

"Somebody once called me a sissy for being polite, but it isn't true. There's a 'man' in 'manners.'"

—Elvis Presley

"People get it wrong. I mean, we've been called that word 'macho'—that's not even in my fucking dictionary. What does it mean?"
—Angus Young, AC/DC, 1982

"Chicks all dig the Wolf. They *all* dig the Wolf. Because he is a mighty Wolf, he's a mountain Wolf, he wipes out his tracks."

—Howlin' Wolf, 1966

WHAT'S IT ALL ABOUT?
(MEANINGS AND MESSAGES)

"There's shitloads of meaning in the songs. I don't know what they mean, but there's still meaning there. They mean things, but I just don't exactly know what."

—Liam Gallagher, Oasis, 1996

"Message songs, as everybody knows, are a drag...Myself, what I'm going to do is rent Town Hall and put about 30 Western Union boys on the bill. I mean, then there'll *really* be some messages. People will be able to come and hear more messages than they've ever heard before in their life."

—Bob Dylan, 1966

"We don't want to sit around and get depressed, though. Life is a joke. Every time you turn on the radio you hear about a murder and some of them are funny. That's what we sing about."

—Johnny Ramone, 1977

"We're in awe of being, essentially. That's where those lyrics are coming from—the inability to go, 'This is my nose, these are my cheeks, it's now 5:30, 1987, in the World.'"

—Curt Kirkwood, Meat Puppets, 1987

"There's a scene in *Last Tango in Paris* where Brando says, 'I don't need to talk but we can still communicate.' And he grunts and groans. That's pretty similar to what I achieve."

—Gary Glitter

"Eventually I would like to reach the stage where I didn't have to write about love and kisses and all that stuff. I wish I could write about really ultimate things. That's where I think all of us want to go, really. All the groups seem to be heading towards a kind of pop music which deals with ultimate things."

—Eric Burdon, the Animals, 1968

"I do know what my songs are about. Some are about four minutes, some are about five, and some, believe it or not, are about eleven or twelve."

—Bob Dylan, 1966

"Taste is a thin line. We sing about glue and all that; we feel that's within taste. You can sing a song about pinheads because there are no pinheads; you don't see any pinheads."

—Johnny Ramone, 1980

"What the music says may be serious, but as a medium it should not be questioned, analysed, or taken so seriously. I think it should be tarted up, made into a prostitute, a parody of itself. It should be the clown, the Pierrot medium. The music is the mask the message wears—music is the Pierrot and I, the performer, am the message."

—David Bowie, 1971

"Those Bob Dylan days are over. You can't just go out there and tell it like it is, but we subtly stick things in there now and then."

—Jon Anderson, Yes, 1988

"My real message? Keep a good head and always carry a light bulb."

—Bob Dylan, 1965

"My motto? The angle of incidence equals the angle of reflection."

—Ric Ocasek, the Cars, 1979

"I don't think music is meant to be understood that much. These guys get up on stage, and they get down, and they rock out, and you're supposed to rock your butt back and forth, and take drugs and alcohol, and smooch with your sexual partner, and then go out and break things after the show."

—Curt Kirkwood, Meat Puppets, 1986

"We shouldn't be penalized for having ideas."

—Gerald Casale, Devo, 1980

MY NAME IS BILL AND I'M A HEAD CASE
(MENTAL HEALTH)

REPORTER: Do you believe in lunacy?
RINGO STARR: Yeah, it's healthy.
REPORTER: But aren't you embarrassed by all the lunacy?
RINGO: No, it's crazy.

—1964

"Pop people are defects. Pop people are funny in the head and the more pop they get, the funnier their heads become. Pop begins in bedrooms and ends up in supermarkets."

—Damon Albarn, Blur

"I've a theory that all creative acts—whether they're painting, writing music, anything—are conducted in a state of madness, which is basically the unconscious mind unleashed. That's what Zodiac is."

—Mark Manning, Zodiac Mindwarp, 1986

"Am I schizophrenic? One side of me probably is, but the other side is right down the middle, solid as a rock."
—David Bowie, 1976

"Who wants to hear about Brian's mental problems anyway? I mean, to call a record 'Sweet Insanity,' imagine that. A whole album of Brian's madness that no one wants to release and still everyone says he's a genius! I make 'Kokomo,' it goes to number one in the charts, and I'm still the dumb, know-nothing, talentless Mike Love."

—Mike Love, Beach Boys, 1995

REPORTER: How do the Beatles keep their psychic balance?
GEORGE HARRISON: There's four of us, so if one goes a little potty, it's all right.

—1964

"I think I was the genius of the group. At least that's what the psychiatrists tell me."

—Dee Dee Ramone, 2001

TV PARTY TONIGHT!
(MULTI-MEDIA)

"I don't even use the word 'video.' Sometimes it will slip out, but I prefer to say 'film' or 'promotional device.'"

—Morrissey, 1987

"One thing that makes me very aware of middle America is the way talk shows treat certain individuals and their circumstances. You know, the kind of people you see on *Hard*...uh, *Current Copy*...*Lurid Affair*...whatever they're called."

—Eddie Vedder, Pearl Jam, 1994

N.M.E.: How much of your time do you devote to music these days?
CHUCK BERRY: I spend about 40% of my time on music.
N.M.E.: And the rest?
BERRY: I have some other businesses back home.
N.M.E.: What are they?
BERRY: Video.
N.M.E.: Video?
BERRY: That's right.
N.M.E. What kind of things are you doing with video?
BERRY: You know what video is?

—1976

"Why must we do the interview on the night of 'Mission Impossible,' man? That's a helluva good program. That's a great show, man. I don't know what day it comes on because I don't watch television that much. I'm one of those phonies that says he doesn't watch it, but watches it every night."

—Phil Spector, 1969

"Now that the burning question of Madonna's virginity has been answered, we are free to go on to even more *gaping* questions— such as, 'How is a video made?'"

—Bette Midler, first MTV Awards, 1984

"The thing that sticks in my mind about meeting Elvis is that he had the first remote switcher for a telly I'd ever seen. And he was switching channels! We were like, 'How are you doing that?'"

—Paul McCartney, 2000

"If you wanted to torture me you'd tie me down and force me to watch our first five videos."

—Jon Bon Jovi, 1987

"We don't do photo sessions anymore. We had physical dummies, replicas of ourselves made. They are plastic and more resistant to photographs."

—Ralf Hutter, Kraftwerk, 1983

INTO THE MYSTIC
(MYSTICISM)

"I used to levitate on stage but a lot of that was chemical, I think."

—Julian Cope, the Teardrop Explodes

"The Giant is inside everyone—as long as you let your trust and your pride go by the wayside, something will happen that will bring the Giant out."

—Larry Gowan, 1987

"I have a clairvoyant woman that I go and see, and she told me that in my last lifetime I was a Mohican Indian and I had my brain removed."

—Peter Gabriel, 1974

"In the studio it's more of a private meditational type of discipline, a sort of searching within oneself to solve problems, to

understand what to express—not necessarily musically—and to end up feeling satisfied with what comes out. That in itself is another kind of learning process, just in the same way cathartic psychotherapy of live events is one form of communal learning process."
—Genesis P-Orridge, Psychic TV, 1985

"How I got to be a psychedelic guru was I just appointed myself one. Basically, all you have to do to become one is take enough drugs."
—Lux Interior, the Cramps, 1980

"I asked a Ouija board once if I'd ever be in a rock band. It said no and I was crushed."
—Fred Schneider, B-52's, 1980

"We can fly, you know. We just don't know how to think the right thoughts and levitate ourselves off the ground."
—Michael Jackson

"The stars are matter, we're matter, but it doesn't matter."
—Captain Beefheart, 1971

"Well, working on the theory of infinity—which has been proven to be wrong for the universe—but let's imagine for a second, for the sake of the question, that the universe goes on for infinity, and look at the probability. That means that the chances of us being here are one in infinity, therefore there's an infinite chance that there's an infinite number of planets just like this one."
—Clive Jackson, Doctor and the Medics, 1991

"I was outside the canopy of the Earth, past the planets and into the stars, juiced up by some cosmic petrol pump attendant."
—Julian Cope, the Teardrop Explodes

PUFFY-PUFFY BO-PUFFY, BANANA-FANA FO-FUFFY, FE-FI MO-MUFFY...P. DIDDY?
(NAMES)

"We were over at Jeff Porcaro's house watching *The Wizard of Oz*. We wanted to use a two-syllable name for the band, something simple. Toto seemed just right. Toto means 'everything' in Latin, 'little boy' in Swahili, and 'Betty' in German. Mind you, we didn't know that at the time we made the decision."

—David Hungate, Toto, 1979

"I'm going by the name of P. Diddy right now on this album. We're doing the next level of flava, but you know I'm not crazy with the name change. You can still call me Puffy."

—Puff Daddy, 2001

"Led Zeppelin is a good name, isn't it? I made it up. Everybody says Keith Moon made it up, but he didn't."

—John Entwistle

TOMMY SMOTHERS: And over here, the guy who plays the sloppy drums. What's your name?
KEITH MOON: Keith. My friends call me Keith, but you can call me John.

—"The Smothers Brothers Comedy Hour," 1967

"First we were going to call the band Drunk Cops, and we put it on a flyer and I woke up in the morning and realized that was really bad. I called the other guys and said we couldn't be Drunk Cops, so we said, 'Okay, we'll be Wall of Voodoo.' After six months it sounded perfect."

—Stan Ridgway, 1989

"My name's got 'evils' and 'lives'. It's probably better not to wonder too much about it."
—Elvis Presley, 1969

"People love our name. It is not a dumb name."
—Marc Storace, Krokus, 1981

"If the Beatles hadn't been good, that name would have sounded stupid."
—Fred Durst, Limp Bizkit, 2001

"Certainly couldn't call [*Nashville Skyline*] *Lay, Lady Lay*. I wouldn't have wanted to call it that, although that name was brought up. It didn't get my vote, but it was brought up. *Peggy Day—Lay, Peggy Day*, that was brought up. A lot of things were brought up. *Tonight I'll Be Staying Here With Peggy Day*. That's another one. Some of the names just didn't seem to fit. *Girl From the North Country*. That was another title which didn't really seem to fit. Picture me on the front holding a guitar and *Girl From the North Country* printed on top."

—Bob Dylan, 1969

"Have you ever tried to name a band? *Every conceivable name* is tied up by copyrights, from Psychedelic Strawberries to Incredible Warthog. Toto is such a simple name, no one ever thought of using it."

—David Hungate, Toto, 1979

"Not to my knowledge have I talked with this person of whom you spoke—Dick Jagger?"

—Chuck Berry, 1969

"Kids gave me the name Bo Diddley in school. I got the nickname because I took up for little guys who couldn't defend themselves. I was raised in Chicago, and you either had to learn how to be a fast runner after school or be fast with your hands. Be fast on your feet, or have a good gift of gab. Later, when I got old enough to go into the gym, I started hanging around and learning boxing. We'd all beat up on each other, and it was good. Anyway, they started calling me Bo Diddley. Don't ask me why."

—Bo Diddley, 1988

"A bread truck came along right at the time we were trying to think of a name. We had been saying, 'How about Bush, Telephone Pole? Ah, bread truck—Bread.' It began with a B, like the Beatles and the Bee Gees. Bread also had a kind of universal appeal. It could be taken a number of ways. Of course, for the entire first year people called us the Breads."

—David Gates, 1988

"After this album I'm going to call myself Billy Ocean. I'm going to do a solo album under his name and everything!"

—Andre 'Dre' Benjamin, Outkast, 2001

WE DIG SNOW AND THE RAIN AND THE BRIGHT SUNSHINE
(NATURE)

"Water represents a lot of stuff. Power—water brings electricity. And it cleanses. Water gives life, and it can take away life. And then when you want to show off, you do like Jesus and walk on it."
—M.C. Hammer, 1994

"Scientists think that we are a super-advanced race compared to trees, but maybe we're not. Maybe the trees have gone through the same trip as we have and have finally perfected themselves into a form where they don't want and don't need to have things."
—Jon Anderson, Yes, 1973

"Everything's breaking down, falling apart. The ozone layer, polar ice caps are melting…it's so overwhelming, really."
—Mick Hucknall, Simply Red, 1987

"I never liked to tread on the grass. I always thought it would automatically kill it. But then somebody told me it usually bounces straight back up, so I don't feel so bad about it now."
—Natalie Merchant, 10,000 Maniacs, 1989

"You know, they've found a use for cockroaches and it's pretty good. What it is is that they predict earthquakes by their behavior. Is that hip? I knew they were worth it. They are beautiful things."
—Captain Beefheart

"When I was small I dug for worms, but I didn't use no map. When it rained, I'd get a jar, put 'em in a jar, close the jar, poke holes in the top for air, and keep 'em as pets. But they always dried up and died. Sad life, I tell ya."
—Cyndi Lauper, 1986

"Never let a photographer take you outside. That just means he has a tree he wants to take a picture of and he needs someone to stand in front of it."
Paul Westerberg, 1995

"While walking across America, I'd listen to different species of birds. If I imitated them, they stuck around."
—Art Garfunkel, 1997

"My mother used to take me out to the fields to teach me bird calls."

—Joni Mitchell, 1974

"You can call it boasting, but that's spirit, that's power. God boasts every day. Every time you see the sun, every time you see the moon, God is showing you his power. Thunder. Lightning. That's nature boasting because nature is perfection."

—L.L. Cool J, 1992

"There's a toxic waste dump behind my house, and my cat's growing a second head."

—Chan Marshall, Cat Power, 1998

HEAVEN KNOWS I'M MISERABLE NOW
(NEGATIVITY)

"I'm disgusted with the government. I'm disgusted with the police force. I'm disgusted with my life. I'm disgusted with my friends' lives. It sounds negative, but you know me—I'm negative, but not that negative."

—John Cougar Mellencamp, 1989

"We're not mean, but a lot of people in the public eye want people to think they're a wonderful person. We have never set out to make people think that we're wonderful people. Quite the reverse in many ways."

—Neil Tennant, Pet Shop Boys, 1989

"I've grown very far away from human beings. I like being detached; I don't even like shaking hands. I don't like sweat. I think everyone is ugly. Faces disgust me and feet really make me reek. I think the human body's about one of the most ugly things ever created. It's abysmal."

—John Lydon, 1980

"I like James Taylor personally, and I like his music sometimes...but I don't want to get into who I like; you'll find out how bitter and vile I am."

—Randy Newman, 1973

"When I was three years old, I was very disappointed to open a dictionary and read 'the great auk—extinct.' Now that didn't leave me with much faith in humanity."

—Captain Beefheart, 1988

What matters is that I would never, ever, do anything as vulgar as having fun."

—Morrissey, 1986

OPPOSITES ATTRACT
(ODD COUPLES)

"When I was in school, every weekend I was one of those guys who used to go wherever Jethro Tull was. That's the band to see, if you're going to see a band live. They're all brilliant musicians. Anyone that can play a flute like that, standing on one leg."

—John Tesh, 1997

"Tiffany's my heroine. She's godlike. I *love* that record."

—Elvis Costello, 1989

"Kenny G is sort of somebody you take for granted, but he is a reality. And I'm trying to come to grips with that reality. He's so...what he is. He's so 'I Can't Believe It's Not Butter!' I think there's some truth to the fact that his music is, in fact, darker than any Danzig record."

—Beck, 1996

"We also like Duran Duran a lot. Ever notice how they sound just like Toto? Human League, Culture Club, Flock of Seagulls—we love them all."

—Joey Ramone, 1983

"The only group I believe to go to the lengths we do is the Moody Blues."

—Jim Dandy, Black Oak Arkansas, 1974

"Naturally, I'm a fan of Doris's, but that don't mean I go and see old Doris Day movies. I don't go and see any old movies. In fact, I don't like old anything. 'Cepting of course my old records."

—Sly Stone, 1973

"I'd rather see Liza Minelli than any rock performer."

—Adam Ant, 1982

"My image? Well I think I look more like Peter Noone or David Cassidy than Mick Jagger. I think Noone is very together as an artist and a person. It was wonderful meeting him, actually. And David Cassidy, who I also think is a great performer."

—David Johansen, New York Dolls, 1974

"I'm not that much in love with heavy-metal acid-rock types of groups, although I get along very well with Mick Jagger and Keith Richards and Eric Burdon. They are not as deep as someone like the Zombies or Kiss or something like that."

—Screamin' Jay Hawkins, 1986

"Barry White went to Carver Junior High School, which was not too far from the school I went to. Barry says he used to see me driving down the street and he'd say, 'There goes Richard Berry, and one of these days I'm gonna be singing just like Richard Berry.' I was really flattered, because Barry's a tremendous vocalist. He's got a heck of a version of 'Louie Louie.'"

—Richard Berry, 1986

"I don't care what anybody says—Tammy Bakker is a great singer!"

—Alex Chilton, 1987

"Whew! My God! Country and western music is beautiful. It's been around a long time. I tell you who I used to be crazy about: Roger Miller. There's a nut, man. That cat, man. I used to turn on the radio to hear a tune called 'My Uncle Used to Love Me But She Died.'"

—Wilson Pickett, 1970

"I saw Bob Seger warm up for Kiss in Fort Worth, Texas. So there you have it. It was a moving experience."

—Gibby Haynes, Butthole Surfers, 1987

"I'd love to record with Streisand, that would be good for humanity and for artistic merit."

—James Brown

"10cc were deep. They did some dark tracks."

—Goldie, 1995

"We listen to everything. I remember listening to Morris Day. I like Morris, all he has to do is laugh, he's great. What an attitude. Connie Francis in one of our favorites. That Julio guy, he's amazing."

—Jon Bon Jovi, 1987

"I like the Brady Bunch, but they're perfect in that way no human being is. They look so in touch with the divine. They care about everyone, even Tiger."

—Prince Be, P.M. Dawn, 1993

"Hey, I saw the Moody Blues at the Fillmore East. I took about 20 Dramamines—y'know, that drug for motion sickness? And I saw bananas everywhere, man. It was a real hallucination. If you write this, don't make it sound like they're my favorite group or anything, okay?"

—Dee Dee Ramone, 1983

"My ex-girlfriend told me I absolutely had to buy Motley Crue, *Shout at the Devil*, because it's one of the best records ever made. I have to agree with her. A week doesn't go by now that I don't listen to it."

—Moby, 1997

"The day the Bionic Woman died on 'The Six Million Dollar Man,' that was a tearful day in our household."

—Trent Reznor, Nine Inch Nails, 1995

"Oh yeah, I love Benny Hill. I used to watch him a lot when I was young. I used to love him because it was something your parents never wanted you to see. The bit I liked most was where he used to beat on the little guy with the bald head. Say, whatever happened to Benny?"

—Lil' Kim, 1997

"I wish I'd been more like Ricky Martin, grooving on the Latin thing."

—Joe Strummer, the Clash, 2001

"Don Mahoney, Eddie Money's brother, who's a cop, came out and introduced Eddie, and the brother is so good-looking, I really liked him. Then Eddie Money sang, and he's just great, like a singing John McEnroe. And he's so familiar, like somebody from Max's, that type, I just feel like we know him."

—*The Andy Warhol Diaries*, 1980

"There's more allowed now. I mean, Prince is as interesting a writer as Cole Porter was. They're a lot alike. In the videos, you can see the similarity."

—Randy Newman, 1988

"I like pop records. I like Olivia Newton-John singing 'Magic,' and Donna Summer singing whatever the hell it is she'll be singing. I like the ELO singing 'All Over the World.'"

—John Lennon, 1980

"I used to hate them. I was the guy at the MTV awards who shouted out, 'The Pet Shop Boys suck!' I shouted out during a quiet bit when they played 'West End Girls.' But when I really hate someone I get all their records to try and work out why, and I found I really like them."

—Axl Rose, Guns N' Roses, 1993

"He stayed to the end? Why would he want to do that? Hey! Fancy Axl Rose wanting to be photographed with tragic old us."

—Chris Lowe, Pet Shop Boys, 1993

"I've watched Debby Boone sing 'You Light Up My Life' maybe fifteen, twenty times. Each time... perfect. Each time with total, focused, concentrated commitment to delivering that song. Which I think is real good. Now I ain't a Debby Boone fan, specifically, and I ain't gonna start wearing chiffon dresses tomorrow. But I did learn something by watching that."

—Patti Smith, 1978

CRAZY HORSES
(OSMONDS)

"The Osmonds have a great song about going back to Utah. They had one really heavy record in '73. It's their Sabbath record. It's called *Crazy Horses*. The song's like pounding drums and heavy guitars and a Moog comin' in. The music's really rocking and legitimate. They were plugging into the stuff that was coming out at the time."

—Beck, 1996

"I'm sick of people knocking the Osmonds. I love them for their whole teenybop thing; they're like an American version of the early Beatles."

—Paul McCartney, 1974

ALAN OSMOND: I think we're far from bubblegum. Even Donny, if you listen to his music, there is no way that could be bubblegum.

MERILL OSMOND: Over in Germany we are known as a heavy underground group.

—1973

"As we travelled around we found a lot of young people asking questions, mainly about life. They wanted to know what our philosophies were. Where did I come from? Why am I here? Where am I going? So we decided to put our philosophies in music and we came out with *The Plan*."

—Alan Osmond, 1973

"Interviewers could be pretty mean. In England I was asked, 'How does it feel to be the chubbiest Osmond?'"

—Jimmy Osmond, 1995

"The only thing that hurts is when we have sent a record out to radio stations and they don't tell anybody who it is. They play it and people come in and say, 'Wow, that's heavy, that must be Led Zeppelin or Rod Stewart.' When they hear it's the Osmonds they say ' *Yeugh*, really?' That's what isn't fair. Sometimes people have a tendency to put labels on things, and the labels get in the way of reality."

—Alan Osmond, 1973

"I was brought up as a Mormon, and that's still an important part of my life. I even met Donny Osmond last week."

—Wayne Hussey, the Mission, 1987

CELEBRATION OF THE LIZARD
(PENISES)

"I remember my stepmother was in the kitchen, and I was washing dishes. Every time she said the word *penis*, I'd turn the water on really hard so it would drown out what she said. I thought what she was telling me was horrifying, absolutely horrifying. And I hated the word. I just hated the whole thing."

—Madonna, 1991

"Getting a hard-on on demand would be difficult. That's the thing about hard-ons—the more you want it to get hard, the softer it gets, unless you take a hypnosis course."

—Jarvis Cocker, Pulp, 1996

"I just grab it to be grabbing it. I grab my dick because it's there."

—L.L. Cool J, 1987

"One night, Liz Derringer and I were hanging out with Gene Simmons, and as we were saying goodnight he asked, 'Do you girls want to see my cock dance?' We looked at each other and said, 'Sure.' So he pulled his pants down and proceeded to do this complicated muscle thing he can do. And it danced. I told him he should get it tap shoes."

—Bebe Buell, 1996

"I'm a size queen, right? Honestly, I am. I can't lie. My friends sometimes say, 'You know Janet, it's not always about the size, but the magic in the wand.' And I'm like, 'But there's nothing wrong with a big magic wand.'"

—Janet Jackson, 2001

"Buddy Holly was very big—he had a big Dick Peter, along about 12, 13 inches. When I said he came and went, that's the truth. I'm not saying that to down Buddy, it's not told for that."

—Little Richard, 1987

"I've got a Polaroid of me with my dick out. And it looks good. Quite big. I keep the photo in the *Trainspotting* video box on the shelf. So if anyone's going to burgle my house that's the thing to go for. Sod the Warhols, get the knob shot."

—Robbie Williams, 2000

"Why do people say, 'That has balls'? Because the balls symbolize the power of a man. Don't you love your balls?"

—L.L. Cool J, 1992

"Men should be encouraged to look at each others penises. They needn't be hidden under a bushel."

—Adam Clayton, U2, 2000

"I would love to experience going inside a woman, or standing up and peeing. The functions are fascinating!"

—k.d. lang, 1995

BOB DOLE'S 115TH DREAM
(POLITICS)

"I look more like Nixon than Jagger."

—David Johansen, New York Dolls, 1973

"I think Dylan is the greatest star rock ever produced in the way that he alters people's thinking. I firmly believe that there could never have been a Watergate if it hadn't been for Dylan. Because nobody asked questions before that."

—Ian Hunter, Mott the Hoople, 1974

"If the West, at the end of the Cold War, was supposed to have won the battle between ideologies, if this is the result, then it would have been better to have been Communist, really."
—Thom Yorke, Radiohead, 1999

"If there's anything you don't want, Hoss, is Willie Nelson to be President. I mean, you don't even want him to be Secretary of—you don't even want him to be dogcatcher."
—Waylon Jennings, 1988

"The meaning of the sample is not important—if we have to use communist propaganda we do it, but if we have to use fascist propaganda we will do that as well."
—Daniel B, Front 242, 1989

"When the Russians hear 'Adagio for Strings' by Samuel Barber, they cry their eyes out. He's an American, and here's this American music reducing them to tears. That's subversive politics, man. That's infiltration."
—Billy Joel, 1985

"You know who I like too? Haldeman. He looks just like Robert Wagner. Don't you think Haldeman is a really cool guy?"
—Alice Cooper, 1975

"Who is this DeGaulle? He seems to have gone over bigger'n us."
—Jerry Lee Lewis, 1958

"Gary Hart was pretty well our only hope until he started following his dick around."
—Tesco Vee, the Meatmen, 1987

"The only reason I voted was there was about 10 minutes to go and I came in from a meeting or something, and Lorraine, my wife, said, 'D'you want to go out and vote?' It was such a great evening, and there was something thrilling about arriving with one minute to spare and making a totally worthless gesture."
—Ian McCulloch, Echo and the Bunnymen, 1987

"Nixon, Hoffman, it's the same. They are all from the same period. It was kind of surprising to see Abbie on TV, but it was also surprising to see Nixon on TV. Maybe people get the same feeling when they see me or us. I feel, 'What are they doing there? Is this an old newsreel?'"

—John Lennon, 1980

"And I'd grown up with this thing that the Irish are great, they're our mates, our brothers. We used to joke that Liverpool was the capital of Ireland. Suddenly we were killing our buddies and I thought, wait a minute, this is not clever and I wish to protest on behalf of the people...I did 'Give Ireland Back to the Irish' and was rung up by a lot of people who said, 'Please don't release this. We don't need this right now.' And I said, 'Yes we do. Gotta have it.'"

—Paul McCartney, 1972

"We don't want to write political songs. We don't want to turn our records into speeches."

—Benny Andersson, ABBA, 1976

"He was flamboyant, but, as I talked to him, I sensed that he was a very shy man."

—Richard Nixon on Elvis Presley

"I been friends with presidents! Johnson, Kennedy, Mr. President Habib Bourguida of Tunisia—you know where that is?"

—James Brown, 1986

"I think as long as I'm attacked by the KGB and the CIA, then I'm probably on the right track."

—Joan Baez, 1988

"I don't believe in that word 'can't.' If *you* can't connect me, then transfer me to somebody who can. This is *Sam C. Phillips* calling, and I am *going* to speak to Fidel."

—Sam Phillips, Sun Records, 1960

IT'S ALL TOO BEAUTIFUL
(POSITIVITY)

"I was kind of mean. I'm so glad I'm nice now."

—Patti Smith, 1996

"I write so much positive stuff! Food for thought. Like 'Killer of Giants,' 'Revelation Mother Earth,' 'War Pigs'—I could go on for years."

—Ozzy Osbourne, 1986

"I do love my fellow man, no matter who. Even some Russian guy."

—Dee Dee Ramone, 1983

"Sly and the Family Stone are everyday people. That's beautiful. We are all everyday people. We all work hard. Some of us will never reach the goal financially that we wanted to reach, but we're happy because we're everyday people."

—Little Richard, 1970

"I'm a happy human being—I love life and I love people."

—Celine Dion, 1995

EVEN BETTER THAN THE REAL THING
(PRODUCT PLACEMENT)

"Brian Wilson did one thing during the album that totally astounded me. He loves Diet Coke, and when I tossed him one, he caught it behind his back and popped the top. It was incredible. If I was the president of Coca-Cola, I would want that on film."

—Van Dyke Parks, 1989

"I have fond memories of my association with Coke. They used me to promote their product all over Canada. They figured that they couldn't get a better salesman than Bobby-on-the-spot, and the Coke promotion tied in with all my appearances. We even pioneered playing shopping plazas. Coke followed us wherever we went, and we went everywhere. Only ourselves and Revene the Hypnotist were covering the entire country from Vancouver to Newfoundland in those days."

—Bobby Curtola, 1971

ROLLING STONE: Bob, where is Desolation Row?
BOB DYLAN: Where? Oh, that's someplace in Mexico. It's across the border. It's noted for its Coke factory, Coca Cola machines are—sells—sell a lotta Coca Cola down there.

—1968

"We were the first people to record a jingle that didn't sound like a jingle, one that actually sounded like a song. That started a world trend."

—Bobby Curtola, 1971

"They used 'Spirit in the Sky' in a commercial for American Express. They did a kind of neat thing with it visually...It gave me a lot more faith in American Express, but they still won't give me a card. They gave me money for using it, but not the Gold Card."

—Norman Greenbaum, 1996

GETTIN' IGGY WITH IT
(PUNK)

PLAYBOY: Would you say you still have a rebellious, or punk, quality toward the rest of the world?
BOB DYLAN: Punk quality?
PLAYBOY: Well, you're still wearing dark sunglasses, right?
DYLAN: Yeah.

—1978

"Punk rock is a bad scene, and I don't understand why it has to exist when there's so much in life."

—Frank Sinatra

"Christ was a punk rocker."
—Billy Idol

"When I want to write anthems, I like to listen to the Sex Pistols and Alice to get in the right frame of mind. It's strange because the Pistols were very Alice-influenced. *They* took Alice so far, and now *I'm* taking the Pistols somewhere else."

—Dee Snider, Twisted Sister, 1984

"Being 17 and in a hardcore band is just about the pinnacle of human experience."

—Lou Barlow, Dinosaur Jr., 1987

"I understand why punk has that aggressive tone, but I don't appreciate it as music. When we grew up, we were quite well off, so there was never any need to be so rebellious. We have a high standard of living in Sweden, so really punk rock is more like a fashion there."

—Björn Ulvaeus, ABBA, 1982

"We're not into sweet harmonies or anything like that."

—Cheetah Chrome, Dead Boys, 1978

"We got over the Sex Pistols. The Sex Pistols couldn't play and Johnny Rotten couldn't sing. Who would dare say that that is part of rock 'n' roll? Who bought those dreadful records?"
—Cliff Richard, 1992

"Punk's like the Rolling Stones were for us when we were kids. Remember when they first did that song, 'Let's...er...Go to Bed Together'? That was like, wow, big stuff."

—Pia Zadora, 1986

"People remember that I'm the guy responsible for all these creeps hanging around now. Someone the other day called me the grandfather of punk. I mean, father maybe, but fucking grandfather? I'm still the best around and that's why I keep going. I'm like a gunfighter: every time I'm about to put my leathers away, there's always some punk band that thinks they're better. I love the challenge."

—Alice Cooper, 1980

"If I was a punk, I'd kill myself."

—Rory Gallagher, 1979

"Listen, I was the originator of punk rock. We had a big sign on the Sunset Strip that read, 'The Cosmic Punk,' and no one got it."

—Marc Bolan, T. Rex, 1977

"Thank God I didn't invent anything as banal as punk rock. It's high-school prom crossed with pub rock."

—Iggy Pop, 1999

"It takes more than bad playing to make a good punk band. You've got to be talented and genuine, like us."

—Tommy Ramone, 1977

"The Sex Pistols arrived in the U.S. today. Punk is going to be so big. They're so smart, whoever's running their tour, because they're starting in Pittsburgh where the kids have nothing to do, so they'll go really crazy."

—*The Diaries of Andy Warhol*, 1977

I LOOK ALL WHITE BUT MY DAD WAS BLACK
(RACE)

"I want to paint the picture for you. It's the 1960s. The college campus is in a militant atmosphere. Everybody's saying, 'Black Power!' Everyone's going to the Panther meeting because H. Rap Brown's in town. And I'm going to play tennis in all whites! Listen to me, man. You understand where I'm coming from? The weirdest!"

—Lionel Richie, 1996

"That phone call a minute ago, that was Fats Domino on the way over. He's one of the great talents in the world. So is Little Richard, but he has problems. 'I'm not a Negro,' he says. 'I'm an Indian.'"

—Jerry Lee Lewis, 1974

"When I would go to Madison Square Garden, I'd have about 35,000 whites and about 50 black people in the audience. In the whole place. But it didn't make no difference. A scream and a holler's a holler to me. I just love 'em. These were my fans and I loved 'em and they loved me, too. So it was a hand for a hand and a foot for a foot. And a pot on a pot. *Bom bom*!"

—Little Richard, 1984

"I know some people accuse us of singing white, but it makes me laugh...People sing styles. They don't sing colours."

—Ron Townson, the 5th Dimension, 1970

"When I first heard Jimi Hendrix, I figured there's like the Charlie Parker of the guitar. I mean, I enjoy being white and stiff and boogeying in that particular way as well, but there are moments when I would really just like to fly like that."

—Pete Townshend, 1972

"I just don't understand white people. White people like stuff that is so overtly wack: Soul Asylum, Rush, *Sports Illustrated*."

—Mike D, Beastie Boys, 1994

"I've never really had a problem with white people at all. There's a few of course, every bunch, a few rejects. But that's with every race. That's a human thing."

—KRS-One, 1995

"We just ain't funky dudes. Finally, I'm just totally proud of the music I listen to—of not going through life embarrassed and really wishing I'd listened to James Brown records when I was 14. I'm very happy I used to listen to Led Zeppelin."

—Billy Duffy, the Cult, 1987

"I went through a period of time when I had a problem with both white kids and black kids, for different reasons. I just said, 'Fuck the both of you. I'm green.'"

—Terence Trent D'Arby, 1989

"When everything ends and the culture is bankrupt, beige is the colour of resignation and acceptance."

—Beck, 1996

"I try not to look at it that way. Being white. I don't wake up every day and look in the mirror, 'Oh. I'm white.'"

—Eminem, 2000

KENNY: Well, we think the Wu-Tang Clan may be a little too...*urban*.
ARTIE: Urban? Well, I can call my good friend Lenny Kravitz. He's only *half* urban.

—"The Larry Sanders Show," 1998

"You want to know why they went after 2 Live Crew? It's a racial thing. It has nothing to do with them being dirty, it has to do with them doing shows in Miami where there's 20,000 white girls screaming 'Me so horny.'"

—Ice-T, 1995

"Everybody's colored or else you wouldn't be able to see them."

—Captain Beefheart, 1970

QUEEN LATIFAH APPROXIMATELY
(RAP)

"Back in the day, we called ourselves NUSKOOL (New Underground Systematically Killin' Old Lyrics). I rapped every day. My life was a big-ass rap tour for no money."

—Coolio, 1995

"One time I did a show where I didn't do the nasty rap. It was for Aaron Spelling, who's a big L.A. producer—he does 'Dynasty' and all that. I'm in this room with all these millionaires, and I didn't do no nasty raps. These three 50-year-old white women took me to the coat room and they said, 'Ice-T, what happened to your erotic rhyme? My daughter comes to your club every Friday night, and she said you have the most splendid sexual rhyme.'"

—Ice-T, 1995

"I tried to breakdance. I couldn't breakdance. Tried to hop. I couldn't hop. I was all right, but I wasn't tight like the other motherfuckers. They could bust nine spins, but I could only do two or three. So I was like, 'Fuck that. I ain't fucking with that. I'll just rap.'"

—Snoop Doggy Dogg, 1995

"There's a revolution going on in white households. Kids who used to listen to Stray Cats or Adam Ant, now they've got Ice Cube and Public Enemy posters. Their fathers are saying, 'Whoa! What's going on? Why are you dressing like this? Why are you listening to that?'

101

And the kids are saying, 'Yo, we ain't rolling like you used to roll.' You know what I'm saying?"

—Ice Cube, 1995

"I was in Maui recently, and I was thinkin', 'Wow, this'd be a really nice place to live,' but I probably couldn't rap no more 'cause what am I gonna rap about? Palm trees, fish, and the deep blue sea? I'd have to start paintin' or something."

—Ice-T, 1995

MUTINY ON THE BOUNTY'S WHAT WE'RE ALL ABOUT
(REBELLION)

"As you know, we are the world's most dangerous group."

—Eazy-E, N.W.A., 1991

"My image had been so white bread, so milkshake, and *Grease* was a chance to do something different...It proved to be so important for me. It meant I could have a hit movie with hit songs and a new image. Suddenly, if I wanted to be outrageous, I could. If I wanted to sing rock 'n' roll, I could. Had it not been for *Grease*, I don't know if I ever could have gotten away with 'Let's Get Physical.'"

—Olivia Newton-John, 1988

"The grungiest thing I did all week was pull the tablecloth out from under four place settings and they all stayed there."

—Evan Dando, the Lemonheads, 1993

"When I go into a new town sometimes, I wonder if the police will shoot me."

—Wendy O. Williams, the Plasmatics, 1981

"I'm not concerned about being an established performer. Mothers still hide their kids from me in airports, and the rumors are still hot and heavy."

—Alice Cooper, 1980

"Prison would probably be the making of me. It would be the beginning of life. I'd probably prosper. We all need a bit of restriction."

—Morrissey

"Are we subversive? That would depend on who's using the word. I'm sure Jerry Falwell would see us as subversive, and that's good."

—Gerald Casale, Devo, 1982

"About the closest thing that Willie ever did to bein' an outlaw is that he probably came to town and double-parked on Music Row."

—Waylon Jennings, 1988

"Rasta music is militant to shake up Babylon. I see even the Pope a Rasta number-one enemy. You know that?"

—Michael Rose, Black Uhuru, 1982

"We like playing with extremes."

—Tim Finn, Split Enz, 1981

"Remember, we were only famous for four years, so most of the world didn't get to see us, and then only on TV, and that was toned down. Madonna and Michael Jackson can grab their crotches on MTV, but we couldn't in those days. Now we're crazy on stage."

—Felipe, the Village People, 1994

"Bad language isn't second nature to me, it's first. Bad language and bad behaviour. It's a fucking winning combination, you've got to admit."

—Ozzy Osbourne, 1997

"Denuding yourself in front of one thousand people is basically saying, this is as far as I can go."

—Julian Cope, the Teardrop Explodes, 1982

"We went to Hamburg. The promoter told us beforehand: 'If they don't like you, they'll run you off the stage.' I said: 'No one runs us off the stage.' The show starts. I look out into the audience and the place is filled with leather boys. Some of these guys were sixty years old! I mean these were not day trippers—they had leather up the ass! Then I notice this one leather boy in front of the stage, and he looks like he's the toughest one of all. He's orchestrating the whole group. He's controlling them, wielding a cat o' nine tails. They didn't bother us at all. We did a great show. I love being scared."

—Wendy O. Williams, the Plasmatics, 1981

"Artists are meant to put their finger on something society hasn't figured out yet. In a way, artists are meant to be the enemies of society. Society is very structured, and our job is to rattle that cage for better or worse; generally we're supposed to be sort of outlawish."

—Huey Lewis, 1992

"Frankly, I didn't see the Rolling Stones until the day before the broadcast. They were recommended by my scouts in England. I was shocked when I saw them. Now, the Dave Clark Five are nice fellows. They are gentlemen and they perform well. It took me seventeen years to build this show. I'm not going to have it destroyed in a matter of weeks."

—Ed Sullivan, 1964

THE WORDS TO A SERMON THAT NO ONE WILL HEAR
(RELIGION)

"I'm a latent Puritan. I used to be an altar boy and all that stuff, Lutheran, and I still have some sense of right and wrong."

—Arthur Kane, New York Dolls, 1973

"When I was younger I wanted to be the Pope. That's typical of me—I immediately go on a power trip. But I also wanted to be a ballet dancer."

—Neil Tennant, Pet Shop Boys, 1993

"If my music career didn't take off, I would've become a nun."

—Christina Aguilera

"The Catholics in Britain and America have the *worst* music. If you're a Church of England member or a Protestant, then you have very lovely hymns. But the Catholics have these terrible hymns...Or even worse they have these folk masses with people playing guitars and flutes, and that *really*...I find that unbearable."

—Neil Tennant, 1994

"Crucifixes are sexy because there's a naked man on them."

—Madonna, 1985

"A lot of Christians are really good to people, and I think that's brilliant. I think it's great to be nice."

—Chris Martin, Coldplay, 2000

20-WAY TIE FOR LAST
(SELF-DEPRECATION)

"One more hit and we're the most successful girl group of all time. Well past the Supremes. Sad, isn't it?'"
—Sarah Dallin, Bananarama, 1988

"I don't know anything about music. In my line, you don't have to."
—Elvis Presley

"I went to see *Spinal Tap* and I didn't think it was funny. I thought it was a fucking documentary, I did."
—Ozzy Osbourne, 1997

"Right now people think I'm ugly, but in 150 years they might think I'm handsome."
—Tom Delonge, Blink 182, 2000

DICK CLARK: Why is so much happening in San Francisco these days, have you figured that out?
JIM MORRISON: Uh...the West is the best, I guess!
—"American Bandstand," 1967

"We've proved that you don't have to be interesting to be an okay band."
—Michael Stipe, R.E.M., 1982

"If you want mumbled garbage, you've come to the right place."
—Jon Langford, Mekons, 1985

"There must be something good about *Tubular Bells*, but I can't quite put my finger on it."
—Mike Oldfield

"I was born to be socially inept."
—Neil Hannon, the Divine Comedy, 1997

"We're influenced by so many things. You could say I'm the Ray Coniff of the pop world."

—Elton John, 1973

"We never said we were brilliant."

—Billy Duffy, the Cult, 1987

"We're definitely not afraid of repeating ourselves. We've earned the right to repeat ourselves because we've done so very little. I don't know. I even like moustaches, so I'm not too good a judge of what sounds like what."

—Curt Kirkwood, Meat Puppets, 1986

"You should hear our version of 'Louie Louie'—wow."

—Ian Curtis, Joy Division, 1980

"'Music Sounds Better With You' took maybe a week to make, I don't know. The more people who say it was made in two seconds, the happier I am."

—Thomas Bangalter, Daft Punk, 1999

"How can you communicate to an audience when you look like a parrot?"

—Tim Finn, Split Enz

FRANK PAGE: I'd like to know how you came up with that rhythm and blues style. Because that's all it is.

ELVIS PRESLEY: Well, sir, to be honest, we just stumbled upon it.

—"The Louisiana Hayride," 1954

"Everything I've ever said is rubbish. I've talked enough rubbish to fill one of those huge refuse tips down on the Thames. There's been the odd time when by pressure of numbers, law of averages, I've said something intelligent, but that would be like trying to find a body in the refuse tip."

—Joe Strummer, the Clash, 1988

"We can definitely brag about our Scrabble. I think we can pretty much take down any other rock band."

—Stephen Malkmus, Pavement, 1999

"I really have got massive problems with myself."
—Siobhan Fahey, Bananarama, 1994

"If the Dolls did one thing, we singlehandedly lowered the standards of an entire industry."
—David Johansen, 1979

YOU SAY NEATO, CHECK YOUR LIBIDO
(SEX)

"My whole gay activities were really into masturbation. I used to do it six or seven times a day. In fact, everybody used to tell me that I should get a trophy for it."
—Little Richard, 1984

"Everything I've ever loved was immoral, illegal, or grew hair on your palms."
—Steven Tyler, Aerosmith

"You have to get people's attention is some kind of way. But I'm not just sex, sex, sex."
—Donna Summer, 1978

"I used to go out with this boy who did not and *would* not perform oral sex. Clearly he wasn't a real man, because, I'm sorry, a real man gives head."
—Shirley Manson, Garbage, 1996

"It hasn't always been like this. They didn't use to write on my school reports, 'Jarvis could do better in this subject...and he's a sex god.'"
—Jarvis Cocker, Pulp, 1996

"Britney would make a better prostitute than Christina—she's thicker."
—Snoop Doggy Dogg, 2001

"I don't think I'd like it if everyone was walking around naked all the time. I like clothes. But I think everybody should run naked through the street at least once. Or be naked when you're not supposed to be naked. It's very liberating."
—Madonna

"I didn't know you could beat off until 1972."

—Ted Nugent, 1980

"All 'Whip It' was, was a self-help song, but they never listen to the words."

—Gerald Casale, Devo, 1982

"You can waggle your codpiece or masturbate with the flute if you're playing a bad gig, and if it gets to that, it's not really on anymore."

—Ian Anderson, Jethro Tull, 1977

"With being sexy, you just need a feather, whereas with kinky, you need the whole chicken."

—David Lee Roth, 1986

"There's this thing in America called dates, right? We don't have those in Iceland. People just listen to music, get drunk, and fuck."

—Björk, 1998

"When Bob Dylan sang 'Lay lady lay, lay across my big brass bed,' he didn't mean chicken lay an egg, did he?"

—Samantha Fox, 1987

"Have some class. I don't know how many mothafuckers gonna tell me, 'I'm going to lick you up and down.' If I hear that in one more song..."

—D'Angelo

"Where is there a sexist line in one of my songs? Name one! Even if I do victimize you, it's only because you got dressed up for the occasion. Just like we planned..."

—David Lee Roth, 1986

"You know, they made a survey and found out that 70% of all records are now sexually oriented. If you listen you'll hear sex in nearly every damn thing. Even Helen Reddy had a song out— 'Make Love to Me.' Boy, that was hot stuff."

—Hank Ballard, 1981

"Patti Smith or Olivia Newton-John...they're me two favorites. I could pull 'em any night."

—Phil Lynott, Thin Lizzy, 1977

"I think I do OK—I've got a certain appeal—but I don't think I'm particularly sexy. I see myself in the mirror first thing in the morning and it's not too good...The voice is working great, though, and the 'old boy' is working pretty well too, so everything's pretty good actually."

—Rod Stewart, 2001

"I was just thinking, are the Spice Girls the Anti-Christ? That's the way it feels to me, though there's a big controversy in America right now about them, about them being tantamount to a porno act, and the religious right—which is neither—have come out very vehemently opposed to them, saying that if children watch their videos they are watching a pornography film. Well, I disagree with that because there's a big difference between a Spice Girls video and a porno film...Some porno films have pretty good music."

—Phil Spector, 1998

"I'm, like, obsessed with pornography. Period. Hardcore, anything. Except for child pornography. It would have to be adults. More than two adults. Ed Powers has this series called *Dirty Debutantes*...There are a thousand of them. I own volumes one to nine hundred."

—Prince Be, P.M. Dawn, 1998

CREEM: What kind of birth control do you use?
DEBORAH HARRY: Let's get back to music.

—1979

"AIDS kinda sucks. We ain't diggin' it."

—Taime Downe, Faster Pussycat, 1987

"Pussy! Money and pussy! Anything besides that's irrelevant!"

—D.J. Yella, N.W.A., 1991

"Do you know I've never slept with a German? I think that's quite weird. I was going to write a song about that: 'I've Never Had a German'!"

—Boy George, 1989

"When I walk by a construction site, the hardhats can't believe their eyes. They ring all the bells. They beep all the beepers."
—Wendy O. Williams, the Plasmatics, 1981

"The problem is that I've explored about every avenue of sex that I've heard of, OK? The trouble is that I like 'em, most of 'em. I'm not too fond of the bathroom trips, but aside from that, in the catalog of sexual history I think that there are very few things that I don't like."
—David Crosby, 1970

"We named Richard Manuel 'The Gobbler.' He's a housewrecker, man, a working girl's favorite and a housewife's companion, if you know what I mean."
—Ronnie Hawkins, 1969

SPIN: "How did you lose your virginity?"
L.L. COOL J: "I had sex."
—1987

WHERE'S THAT CONFOUNDED BRIDGE?
(SONGWRITING)

"You can write blues songs in no time. 'Baby please don't go/Baby please don't go/I love you so/Baby please don't go.' What's to that?"
—Chuck Berry, 1986

"'Gangsta's Paradise,' I had to change the lyrics on that so many times to get the sample clearance. Stevie Wonder wasn't clearing nothing with cursing! I even had to change 'Mack 10' to just '10'!"
—Coolio, 1995

"I heard some Beatles stuff on the radio the other day, and I heard 'Green Onion'—no, 'Glass Onion,' I don't even know my own songs!"
—John Lennon, 1980

"It's a little galling now to find that I own less of 'Yesterday' than Michael Jackson! It's a thorn in my side, and I keep thinking I should phone him up. I don't hold a grudge, but if you're listening, Michael, I'll have 'Yesterday' and 'Here, There and Everywhere' back—just for a laugh—and a couple of others."

—Paul McCartney, 1987

"Back in the day, I used to try to make my words rhyme. Like 'cat' would have to rhyme with 'hat.' This time, I really didn't give a fuck because nobody else gives a fuck."

—J-Ro, Tha Liks, 2001

LARRY: Stevie, no, you're misunderstanding me. It's not that I didn't like Beck's music. It's just that he said 'shit' in the middle of one of the songs.
STEVIE: He's an artist.
LARRY: Well, I'm sure 'shit' rhymes with a lot of things.

—"The Larry Sanders Show," 1995

"I write lyrics during the commercials. It took much longer this year because I was watching cable."

—David Lee Roth, 1984

"We're ballbreakers! With most of the ladies who come to clubs, when we go into our ballads we hear, 'Ooooohhh.' But a lot of dudes, bein' players, they don't look at you to sing ballads— 'Yeah, I love that, you doin' real good with that.' Ballads don't attract too many men."

—James "Diamond" Williams, Ohio Players, 1988

"Madonna? Sure, I can appreciate a good Madonna song— I mean, that's sort of what I do, write songs."

—Paul Westerberg, the Replacements, 1987

"You mean they don't realize I'm a songwriter as well as a slut?"

—Madonna, 1989

"If I didn't write about anything but cars, I'd be branded a car guy. Screamin' Jay Hawkins got branded: he sang about ghosts and caskets. You do that, and when nobody wants to hear about ghosts and caskets you're branded."

—Chuck Berry, 1986

"'She Came in Through the Bathroom Window' was written by Paul when we were in New York forming Apple, and he first met Linda. Maybe she's the one who came in the window. She must have. I don't know. Somebody came in the window."

—John Lennon, 1980

"It was the dream of a lifetime. I mean, I'd been going to that BMI dinner since I was a kid. I got six awards in one year, including the Most Performed Song of 1976. 1975, I mean, beating out 'Rhinestone Cowboy.' I was afraid of 'Rhinestone Cowboy.'"

—Neil Sedaka, 1981

"Once you've got the guitar solo, you've only got to write a middle-eight and it's a piece of piss all the way home, man."

—Noel Gallagher, 1997

"I want to say 'bird' or 'bee,' but suddenly I hear words like 'fuck' or 'shit' or 'I'll strangle your mother.'"

—Eminem, 2001

"I had a very hard time trying to present my songs to Lennon and McCartney. George did, too, before me, trying to present his songs. I had a real hard time. It's a bit off-putting when three guys are lying on the floor hysterically laughing as I'm trying to play my song!"

—Ringo Starr, 1992

"I've got no intentions of making any more albums with the Faces. It's too much hard work. Some of the best things I've ever done on their albums have never seen the light of day. I mean 'Silicone Grown,' that one I wrote about silicone tits. I was really proud of that 'cause it's a difficult subject to write about and it just got lost."

—Rod Stewart, 1975

"If you want to write a classic pop song, use these chords: A-flat, B-flat, G-minor 7th, C-minor. You can't go wrong. A guaranteed worldwide hit!"

—Neil Tennant, Pet Shop Boys

"I think a good song for you would be a 55-minute 'Louie Louie.'"

—Iggy Pop, *Metallic K.O.*, 1976

"'Teen Spirit' was such a clichéd riff. It was so close to a Boston riff or 'Louie Louie.' When I came up with the guitar part, Krist looked at me and said, 'That is so ridiculous.' I made the band play it for an hour and a half."
—Kurt Cobain, Nirvana, 1994

"The one time I tried to write a single, it was for Bobby Sherman. Billy Payne and I sat around for hours and 'I need' for a lyric was as far as I got, and the music never got anywhere. We could never find a melody to go with 'I need' and so we quit; as a matter of fact, it was four hours of grueling work. I don't even know what a pop single is, but hell, give me a break."

—Lowell George, Little Feat, 1975

"The words and music to 'Perfect' were written in about 20 minutes and we recorded it, the original demo that's on the album, that same evening. It was overwhelming. I think we finished it around one in the morning and we couldn't leave the studio till about five because...it was pretty scary. I was scared."

—Alanis Morissette, 1999

"I always liked Albania. I've been trying to write a song about Albanians for quite a while, because I think they're funny. More goats than people. A great place. They've always been berserk, though. Their music! It's the craziest stuff you've ever heard."

—Randy Newman, 1973

"I wrote this almost sublime, roaming, guitar-led piece of music once, and the next thing I knew it was called 'Some Girls Are Bigger Than Others.'"

—Johnny Marr, the Smiths, 1996

113

THEY ARE TALKING ABOUT THE SPACE BETWEEN US ALL
(SPIRITUALITY)

"Within the next five years I think I'll be doing something else. As a matter of fact a TM guru told me recently that I was destined to start a big world TM centre in northern California, and that my true vocation in life was that. He said the band was just a prelude to my spiritual destiny, my life as a teacher of TM."
—Mike Love, Beach Boys, 1995

"People have all these weird concepts about each other. They alienate themselves. So part of my mission as a musician or whatever The Creator wanted me to do, was to try to bring the level of humanity up. This is why I write about the things I do."
—Maurice White, Earth, Wind & Fire, 1975

"We also strongly believe in the magic of crystal balls, because when the light falls directly on them, they can possess the power to hypnotize. So we sent out 5,000 quartz crystals to DJs and TV directors all over America, instructing them to hold the crystal with both thumbs and point it toward the centre of the forehead. Then they were to concentrate hard and think about how positive our music is—the warmth of the body excites the molecules in the crystal and they transmit power to the brain. I realize this may sound like a joke, but it's really quite serious, and we were sure that the crystals would help us achieve mega success in the States."
—Barry Gibb, 1988

"My hair is short because it's Guru's will."
—Carlos Santana, 1974

"What *is* a soul? You've got a voice, a big dick, or a fucking top pair of trainers. What's a soul?"
—Liam Gallagher

"I'm just a dog and I'm led around by me collar by Krishna."
—George Harrison

"I find that where I'm from—in America—the total young public is reaching for that now. Everybody is out of drugs, forget

about that, and they're trying to reach a higher form of consciousness. There's a whole new thing now, everyone's involved."
—Maurice White, Earth, Wind & Fire, 1975

LARRY RAMOS: And you know this awareness you were talking about, well, I know a lot of people who are involved in various forms of mysticism at various levels...and it's all part of the same thing. We're going through fantastic changes. Like me, I thought I was a real atheist 'cause I couldn't hang with that crap older people were handing me about religion. But believe me, it's something else now. It's like we created our own church; the church of kids.
TED BLUECHEL: It's beautiful, man!
—The Association, 1968

"Although I can see this world and a horrible situation, I also have a belief in other worlds. I just am a believer of the fairies. I just feel the fairies in my stomach...I *communicate* with the fairies instinctively. I just hear things."
—Tori Amos, 1992

"I'm a poor example of a spiritual person."
—George Harrison, 1979

"But when I looked into Mick's eyes, I saw myself a year ago—a prisoner of the system, playing what the people wanted, not what they needed. I felt it would be wrong to offend him because there's a soul inside that body that wants to be free."
—Carlos Santana, 1974

BEING FOR THE BENEFIT OF TOM KITE
(SPORTS)

"I haven't had sex in eight months. To be honest, I now prefer to go bowling."
—Lil' Kim, 2000

"I'd also like to start a cookbook magazine. And I've always wanted to be a boxing referee. I want to referee a heavyweight championship fight. Can you imagine that? Can you imagine any fighter in his right mind recognizing *me*?"
—Bob Dylan, 1966

"It ends up that every heavy metal guy I know plays golf now, from Motley Crue to Iron Maiden."

—Alice Cooper, 1987

"I could show you a picture of my Pop Warner football team. There were 28 homies on that team. Twelve are dead. Seven are in the penitentiary. Three are smoked out. If they ain't dead or in jail or smoked out, they do the gang thing, sell dope. I can't look at that picture and say, 'Well, hey, he went to college. He got a degree. Hey, that's little Johnnie Cochran.'"

—Snoop Doggy Dogg, 1995

"I think the way to really know what's going on is just being in tune with everything. You can't do it by listening to music. Pro wrestling is real important."

—Rick Rubin, Def-Jam Records, 1985

"I don't like golf courses. They're too consistent in texture, and it bothers me. I'd much rather be in a parking lot."

—Michael Stipe, R.E.M., 1995

REPORTER: What do you plan to do after the breakup of the Beatles?
PAUL McCARTNEY: No one's made any plans, but John and I will probably carry on songwriting, and George will go into basketball.

—1964

"I have a standing offer—and I've told this to Bill and Mike— that if they ever do a charity golf thing again, I will get knickers and a tweed cap and, never having touched a golf club in my life, I will take mushrooms and do a full eighteen holes. As long as it's televised."

—Peter Buck, R.E.M., 1995

"Sports was the only thing I was good at, and I used to love it completely. The 100 metres was my *raison d'etre*. Yes, I won everything. I was a terrible bore when it came to athletics. I was just the type of person everyone despises, so I've carried on in that tradition."

—Morrissey, 1985

SET THE CONTROLS FOR THE HEART OF THE SUN
(TECHNOLOGY)

"The structural dynamics of my pants are a lot simpler than they actually appear to be."

—David Lee Roth, 1986

"Like if the band broke up tomorrow, like if the President declared no more rock 'n' roll music, well, we'd all still be living together as brothers. And right now, we just want to make enough money so that when this computerized society thing is a reality, we can buy our own computer."

—Jim Dandy, Black Oak Arkansas, 1973

"Grand Funk Railroad paved the way for Jefferson Airplane, which cleared the way for Jefferson Starship. The stage was now set for the Alan Parsons Project, which I believe was some sort of hovercraft."

—Homer Simpson, 1996

"I was out there playing, and putting synthesizers on stage and stuff, but when the computers like the Fairlight and that came along, it somehow seemed wrong to me. It seemed too much, too much."

—Gary Numan, 1989

"Anybody could do what I do. Anybody can have a hit record now. It's brilliant."

—Norman Cook, Beats International, 1991

"I can ride everything else, but I hate ferris wheels. I think they are so dangerous."

—Donnie Wahlberg, New Kids on the Block, 1990

JUST THE THREE OF US

"I like to see two women together—it rings my chimes."

—Tom Jones

"I'm pro-heterosexual. I can't get enough of women, and I don't see the same thing that other men can see in men. I'm not into gay or bisexual experiences. But that's hypocritical of me,

117

because I'd rather see two women together than just about anything else. That happens to be my personal, favorite thing."

—Axl Rose, Guns N' Roses, 1989

"Let's not call them orgies, let's just say it was seven or eight people in love."

—Ronnie Hawkins, 1993

"I used to like to watch girls be with girls, you know? I thought that was the most beautiful thing I'd ever seen. I always looked for girls that wouldn't mind doing that. I'm telling you the truth!"

—Little Richard, 1984

A TRUMPET YOU CAN BLOW AND A BOOK OF RULES
(TOOLS OF THE TRADE)

"I don't understand why people think it's so difficult to learn to play guitar. I found it incredibly easy. You just pick a chord, go twang, and you've got music."

—Sid Vicious, 1976

"The next album's going to have some harder guitars. It's going to scare some people because that's what good music does. But they'll eventually come back around and realize that it's innovative."

—Chris Kirkpatrick, 'N Sync, 2001

"You can't make much sense of guitars. They seem a fairly strange instrument. I mean, the idea of six strings, four fingers, one thumb—it makes no sense."

—Ian Marsh, the Human League

"My advice to the amateurs wanting to get into playing the drums is to play the guitar."

—Keith Moon, 1975

"What about these drum machines which can program in mistakes? Program in the human factor? I mean, how human? I know plenty of drummers that aren't that human, you know."

—Elvis Costello, 1989

"Our drummers don't sweat anymore."

—Kraftwerk

"Most guitar bands are just glorified buskers; I've heard people in the subway that are better."
—Scott Walker, 1998

"I'd always played guitar, bass, and drums, and I could honk a bit on a battered old baritone sax, but I got this disease for buying musical instruments. It started when I bought this oboe in a second-hand shop. It was a ridiculously low price. I couldn't play it but I thought, 'Knickers, I'll have it".
—Roy Wood, 1976

"Leslie West of Mountain never gets any recognition. I've always been a fan of his, since back when he was a fat kid dropping out of high school in Forest Hills. He was, to me, one of the top five guitar players of his era. His playing was so soulful and tasteful. His break in 'Theme for an Imaginary Western' is the best thing I've ever heard."
—Johnny Ramone, 1999

"To get your playing more forceful, hit the drums harder."
—Keith Moon

"Everybody was sticking to guitar pop, and we took it to space beats. Now you hear everybody trying to do something digital in their songs."
—JC Chasez, 'N Sync, 2001

"I had no interest in 15-minute guitar solos and whammy bends."
—Mick Hucknall, Simply Red, 1986

"Jangly guitars do not my plunker pull."
—Billy Duffy, the Cult, 1987

"On stage I fuck up a lot because I get so carried away, I forget to put my hands in the right place. Often I'm playing a fret below what it's supposed to be."
—Joe Strummer, the Clash, 1977

119

WATCHERS OF THE SKY
(UFOS)

"When I was young, what we read was the Bible and UFO magazines. Just like I say I'm equal parts Balenciaga and Brando, well, my dad was equal parts God and Hagar the Spaceman in Mega City. My mother taught me fantasy; my mother's like a real hip Scheherazade. Between the two of 'em, I developed a sensibility."

—Patti Smith, 1976

"I used to work for two guys who put out a UFO magazine in England. And I made sightings six, seven times a night for about a year, when I was in the observatory."

—David Bowie, 1975

PAULA: Beck is very original, and I thought it was my job to find fresh, exciting talent for the show.

ARTIE: I'd love to watch him from the mosh pit, and we're in search of fresh faces with a point of view. But not a *hillbilly* from outer space.

—"The Larry Sanders Show," 1995

"I don't see how the tabloids could get any worse for me, unless they claimed I'd had anal sex with an alien, for example: 'Liam Gallagher was caught last night bending an alien across a pool table and poking his bottom.' What more can they say about me?"

—Liam Gallagher, Oasis, 1997

KICKING IN CHAIRS AND KNOCKING DOWN TABLES
(VIOLENCE)

"I'm famous for hitting myself in the face and beating the shit out of myself. Every show, I've got a kid out there who's hitting himself just like me. His knuckles are bloody, his eyes are black. I'll look in his eyes and see that he's in some other place. It's a heavy-duty responsibility."

—Shawn Crahan, Slipknot, 2000

"I have been murderer of the world."

—Howard Devoto, Magazine, 1980

"We did an assassination where someone came out of the audience and shot me. I wear this chest plate with flash pots, gun powder, and condoms full of meat and blood which explode when triggered."

—Ogre, Skinny Puppy, 1985

"I wish that Prince Charles had been shot. I think it would have made the world a more interesting place. But one of them is bound to get it soon. It's on the cards."

—Morrissey, 1996

"I find myself murdering a lot in my more recent dreams. Rugby players, and I don't even know any rugby players. I don't even watch it on television. I don't like it. Maybe that's why I'm murdering them."

—Robert Smith, the Cure, 1986

"In San Antonio back in the '50s, I was just sittin' and not even lookin' at this guy. I was talkin' to a friend, and this guy hauls me off and hits me. Twelve stitches. The women love me, but these damn bruisers—they don't like me at all. I'm stitched up all over."

—Jerry Lee Lewis, 1974

"The only time I remember Dick Clark getting upset was once when someone was guesting on the show, and as they sang, some kid up in the bleachers—who, thank God, was not a regular—throws a penny at the stage. Dick saw it happen and knew where it had been thrown from, but he waited until a station break. Then he climbed up in the bleachers. A deadly silence filled the whole studio. Dick was just *livid*."

—Betty Romantini,
"American Bandstand" dancer, 1984

"Just because I cut the heads off dolls, they say I must hate babies. But it's not true. I just hate dolls."

—Alice Cooper

121

"The Mary Chain used to regularly get their heads kicked in at that time. Them and the Birthday Party just brought out the violence in people."

—Alan McGee, Creation Records, 1995

"I have a beautiful wife, I have three healthy children. I'm happy, man. But when I'm onstage, it's fuckin' ON. I'll kill people. Fuck it. I will look into the eye of the abyss every day of my life, because my time here? It's nothing, man."

—Shawn Crahan, Slipknot, 2000

"I'll tell you who I'd *like* to murder. That bunch of losers, the Dead Boys. 'Specially Stiv Bators...Tell Stiv I'm looking for him and I'm gonna cut him to pieces."

—Sid Vicious, 1978

"I like very much the idea of what I call recycling, of things being reused and put into different contexts. Now, if someone took a big chunk of my work and did something trivial to it and called it theirs, I'd break their legs. Actually, I'd break their fingers first. One by one. "

—Brian Eno, 1992

"I know the fellow that said that. He used to come around here and get beat up all the time. He better watch it; some people are after him. They're going to strip him naked and stick him in Times Square. They're going to tie him up, and also put a thermometer in his mouth."

—Bob Dylan, 1966

"Ice Cube, Eazy-E, and M.C. Ren are great role models. Oderous wants all humans to murder each other—thus, he needs war, famine, pestilence, and he needs Eazy-E."

—Oderous Urungus, Gwar, 1990

SAGE AGAINST THE MACHINE
(THE FINAL WORD)

"Rock stars—is there anything they don't know?"

—Homer Simpson, 1995

Index

* Bold Italic denotes caricatures

Bibliography

Glenn A. Baker, *Monkeemania!* (Plexus, 1986)
Lester Bangs, *Psychotic Reactions and Carburetor Dung* (Knopf, 1987)
Mark Bego, *Madonna: Blonde Ambition* (Harmony Books, 1992)
Victor Bockris and Roberta Bayley, *Patti Smith: An Unauthorized Biography* (Simon & Schuster, 1999)
Jenny Boyd, *Musicians in Tune* (Fireside Books, 1992)
Anthony Bozza and Shawn Dahl (editors), *Rolling Stone Raves* (William Morrow, 2000)
Al Clark (editor), *The Rock Yearbook, 1983* (Virgin Books, 1982)
Caroline Coon, *1988: The New Wave Punk Rock Explosion* (Orbach & Chambers, 1977)
David Dalton, *The Rolling Stones: The First Twenty Years* (Knopf, 1981)
Walli Elmark and Timothy Beckley, *Rock Raps of the '70s* (Drake, 1972)
Colin Escott and Martin Hawkins, *Good Rockin' Tonight* (St. Martin's Press, 1991)
Liz Evans, *Women, Sex and Rock 'n' Roll: In Their Own Words* (Pandora, 1994)
Bill Flanagan, *Written in My Soul* (Contemporary Books, 1986)
Geoffrey Giuliano, *Blackbird: The Life and Times of Paul McCartney* (Dutton/Penguin, 1991)
Geoffrey Giuliano, *The Lost Beatles Interviews* (Dutton, 1994)
Peter Goddard and Philip Kamin (editors), *Shakin' All Over: The Rock 'n' Roll Years in Canada* (McGraw Hill, 1989)
Dan Goldstein, *Rappers Rappin* (Castle Communications, 1995)
Peter Guralnick, *Feel Like Going Home* (Fusion, 1971)
Peter Guralnick, *Last Train to Memphis*(Little, Brown & Company,1994)
Pat Hackett (editor), *The Andy Warhol Diaries* (Warner Books, 1989)
Douglas Kent Hall and Sue C. Clark, *The Superstars in Their Own Words* (Music Sales, 1970)
Kitty Hanson, *Disco Fever* (Signet, 1978)
Chris Heath, *Pet Shop Boys, Literally* (Viking, 1990)
Chris Heath, *Pet Shop Boys Versus America* (Penguin, 1995)
Levon Helm, *This Wheel's on Fire* (William Morrow, 1993)
Nick Hornby, *High Fidelity* (Indigo, 1996)
Barney Hoskyns, *Beneath the Diamond Sky* (Simon & Schuster, 1997)
Maxim Jakubowski, *The Wit and Wisdom of Rock and Roll* (Unwin Paperbacks, 1983)
Alan Light (editor), *The Vibe History of Hip Hop* (Three Rivers, 1999)
J. Marks, *Rock and Other Four Letter Words: Music of the Electric Generation* (Bantam Books, 1968)
Martin Melhuish, *Heart of Gold: 30 Years of Canadian Pop Music* (CBC Enterprises, 1983)
Miles/Andy Mabbet, *Pink Floyd: The Visual Documentary* (Omnibus Press, 1980)

Lucy O'Brien, *She Bop* (Penguin, 1996)
Raymond Obstfeld and Patricia Fitzgerald, *Jabberrock*
(Henry Holt, 1997)
Robert Palmer, *Rock & Roll: An Unruly History* (Harmony, 1995)
Gavin Petrie (editor), *Pop Today* (Hamlyn, 1974)
Bruce Pollock, *When Rock Was Young*
(Holt, Rinehart & Winston, 1981)
Jean-Marie Potiez, *ABBA: The Book* (Aurum, 2000)
Dave Rimmer, *Like Punk Never Happened* (Faber & Faber, 1985)
Jonathan Romney and Adrian Wooton (editors),
Celluloid Jukebox (BFI, 1995)
Bob Sarlin, *Turn It Up (I Can't Hear the Words)* (Touchstone, 1973)
Arnold Shaw, *The Rockin' 50s* (Hawthorn, 1974)
Michael Shore and Dick Clark, *The History of American Bandstand*
(Ballantine Books, 1985)
Joe Smith, *Off the Record: An Oral History of Popular Music*
(Warner Books, 1988)
Jacqui Swift, *Aqua: The Official Book* (Virgin Books, 1998)
Dave Thomas (editor), *Johnny Rotten: In His Own Words*
(Omnibus Press, 1988)
Nick Tosches, *Hellfire: The Jerry Lee Lewis Story* (Delta Books, 1989)
The Philosophy of Andy Warhol (Harvest, 1988)
Marc Weingarten, *Station to Station* (Pocket Books, 2000)
Charles White, *The Life and Times of Little Richard* (Harmony, 1984)
Ritchie Yorke, *Axes, Chops & Hot Licks* (Hurtig Publishers, 1971)
Paul Zollo, *Songwriters on Songwriting* (De Capo, 1997)

Periodicals
Attitude
Beetle
Circus
Creem
Details
Entertainment Weekly
Essence
The Face
Forced Exposure
Gig
Graffiti
Hip-Hop Connection
Hit Parader
Mojo
Music Technology
Nerve!
The New Music
Newsweek

New Musical Express
Option
Penthouse
Playboy
Q
Record Review
Rock Magazine
Rock Video
Rolling Stone
Select
Seventeen
Smash Hits
Sounds
The Source
Spin
Teen People
Trouser Press
Uncut
Vibe

Vibrations
Wet
ZigZag
Zoo World

Online
classicrock.about.com
rocksbackpages.com
eminem2000.com
mtv.com

Movies
annie hall
don't look back
jailhouse rock

TV
"The Simpsons"
"The Larry Sanders Show"

The Editors

Phil Dellio teaches grade 6 at Huttonville P. S., just outside of Toronto. He began writing for *Nerve!* and *Graffiti* in the 1980s, during which time he conducted some of the interviews quoted herein (Martin Degville still doesn't return his phone calls). He has contributed over the years to *popped.com*, *The Village Voice*, *Cinema Scope*, *Innings*, *Tapeworm*, and *Why Music Sucks*, and from 1991 to 1998 he published *Radio On*, a fanzine devoted to Top 40. He was also one of the people interviewed for *Vinyl* (2000), a documentary about record collectors.

As he approaches 40, Toronto record store employee Scott Woods is still figuring out what he wants to be when he grows up. In the meantime, he edits *rockcritics.com* out of his home, and freelances for *The Village Voice* and *DJ Times* in New York and *Eye Weekly* in Toronto.

The Illustrator

Mike Rooth is a graduate of Sheridan College's Interpretive Illustration program, the last class of the 20th century. A St. Catharines native, he now lives in Oakville, Ontario, where he works as a freelance illustrator. Over the past two years his work has appeared in a wide variety of publications, both local and international. This is his first Sound And Vision book.

Other Quotable Books from Sound And Vision

Quotable Alice
Edited by David W. Barber
Illustrations by Sir John Tenniel
isbn 0-920151-52-3

Quotable Sherlock
Edited by David W. Barber
Illustrations by Sidney Paget
isbn 0-920151-52-1

Quotable Opera
Aria Ready for a Laugh?
Edited by Steve Tanner
Illustrations by Umberto Tàccola
isbn 0-920151-54-X

First published in Canada by
Quotable Books
an imprint of
Sound And Vision
359 Riverdale Avenue
Toronto, Canada M4J 1A4

http://www.soundandvision.com
E-mail: musicbooks@soundandvision.com

First edition, September 2001
1 3 5 7 9 11 13 15 - printings - 14 12 10 8 6 4 2

National Library of Canada Cataloguing in Publication Data
Main entry under title:
Quotable pop: five decades of blah, blah, blah
Includes bibliographical references and index.
ISBN 0-920151-50-7
1. Popular music—Quotations, maxims, etc. 2. Rock music—
Quotations, maxims, etc. 3. Musicians—Quotations.
4. Rock musicians—Quotations. I. Dellio, Phil, 1961-
II. Woods, Scott, 1964-
PN6084.R62Q95 2001   781.64   C2001-902001-5

Cover illustration by Mike Rooth
Jacket design by Jim Stubbington
Typeset in Futura

Printed and bound in Canada

A Note from the Publisher

Sound And Vision is pleased to announce the creation of a new imprint called *Quotable Books*. The first three in the series are illustrated on the back cover. Other titles planned include *Quotable Shakespeare, Twain, Wilde, Poe, Blake, Dickens and Quotable Gumshoes.* The series will cover the arts, *Quotable Opera, Quotable Jazz,* and *Quotable Heavy Metal* plus literature and other subject areas, including politicians and statesmen such as Winston Churchill, Oliver Cromwell and Abraham Lincoln.

Our books may be purchased for educational or promotional use or for special sales. If you have any comments on this book or any other book we publish or if you would like a catalogue, please write to us at:

Sound And Vision,
359 Riverdale Avenue,
Toronto, Canada M4J 1A4.

Visit our web site at: www.soundandvision.com. We would really like to hear from you.

We are always looking for suitable original books to publish. If you have an idea or manuscript, please contact us.

Thank you for purchasing or borrowing this book.

Geoffrey Savage
Publisher